A FATHER'S ANGELS

a memoir

A FATHER'S ANGELS

a memoir

John Waldron

HURST BLANDON PRESS

AUTHOR'S NOTE

It would take several years of repeating the same introductory level Spanish class at a Los Angeles area adult education extension program before I no longer broke out into a complete sweat and went blank each time the teacher called my name. Although I eventually progressed to more advanced classes and several immersion trips to further validate my bilingual abilities, my late start at language acquisition forever put me at a disadvantage in my efforts to be fluent in Spanish. With that said, I've made every effort to relay accurate details and events in the writing of this memoir, while truthfully depicting emotions and feelings. Any errors or misrepresentations are unintentional.

More than two years have passed since the Arizona State Legislature enacted Senate Bill 1070. This requires law enforcement officers to request identification from "suspected" immigrants, and makes it a crime to hire or transport an illegal alien. This bill, and others like it, generated fear and resentment throughout the community and led many undocumented people to flee the state. For a dozen years, I hired several women from Mexico to care for my two boys; each was instrumental in furthering my understanding as a parent and father. Along the way, our families became closely interconnected, and at times felt like one. In order to preserve the privacy of these women and their families, as well as my own family and friends, I have changed all names but my own.

CONTENTS

I am eternally indebted to the four women who served as invaluable caregivers to my sons. Never forgotten will be the unconditional love showered upon my boys and the compassion offered to their father.

INTRODUCTION

Just blocks from my home, a demonstration is underway. News crews are in full force—barricades barely separate the two sides and their overwhelming mutual distaste and anger. I stand next to a young father, his small son perched upon his shoulders, and I'm struck by how much this boy resembles what my son, Miguel, looked like more than a decade ago. I can't remember the last time I was able to hoist my two boys upon my shoulders, allowing them a broader worldview. Tonight, this little boy, with his crew cut, beaming dimples, soft brown complexion, and unyielding curiosity is mesmerized by the angry crowd. His tiny hands tightly grip his father's chin as he stares unfalteringly at the sea of angry white faces.

Nearby, a tearful teenage Hispanic girl describes the struggles of her high school friends with a local television reporter. "My friends know nothing else but this country." She explains that they crossed the border illegally with their parents as small children, and were raised and educated in the United States. Soon they'll be deported to a country where they declare no identity or allegiance.

Across the barricades, the insults grow volatile, as more intense, hateful yelling erupts. These gatherings are the direct result of a rising tide of anti-immigration sentiment spreading throughout the nation. The mostly Hispanic crowd is generally peaceful, but determined to protest the increased random sweeps and deportations of undocumented workers. A small but vocal group of mostly white Americans informally gathers on the other side. They speak freely to the reporters, sharing their anger and frustration about the "illegals," while many of the Hispanic protesters are unwilling to go on camera. They're clearly fearful of the overwhelming presence of the law, and rightly so.

As I stand on the periphery and survey the landscape, I struggle to recognize the simmering rage on this street corner. I grew up just a few miles from here, and now raise my family little more than a stone's throw from this emerging epicenter. I hadn't intended to hire an illegal alien, or several for that matter, but standing among the crowd I am certain I'd do it again if faced with the same set of circumstances.

In recent years, Arizona has enacted some of the toughest employer sanction laws, targeting business owners who knowingly hire illegal immigrants. Year after year, flimsily crafted Band-Aid legislation flows through the halls of the Arizona legislature, further restricting employment, healthcare, education, and most other resources that would benefit illegal immigrants and their children. In lieu of any meaningful national solution to the immigration debate, many Arizonans have demanded more vigilant police enforcement. The local county sheriff, Joe Arpaio, self-professed "America's Toughest," is quick to cater to this growing frustration and anger. He carries out frequent raids in-and-around the Phoenix area, where undocumented workers congregate to seek day labor. Handcuffed illegal aliens prove irresistible to local and national media, and as a result have made Sheriff Joe famous.

Many states are following Arizona's lead. Alabama, South Carolina, Georgia, and Indiana have moved forward with similar punitive legislation directed at undocumented workers and their families. In these states, and many others, legislators hope tougher sanctions will send the undocumented back to their homelands, or at the very least somewhere else. The aftermath of such actions has led the U.S. Attorney General to review potential civil rights violations.

There are clear economic ramifications, as well. There is a shortage of manual labor to harvest crops and fill low paying positions within factories and the service industry. In addition, there is a direct impact upon retail sales, and a resulting loss in tax revenues which has negatively impacted municipal and state budgets. In several of these states, families living in fear are too terrified to send their children, many of them American citizens, to school.

Who shall pass through our borders and what skills will they possess? It's estimated by the Department of Homeland Security that there are 11.5 million undocumented immigrants currently residing in the U.S.; more than fifty-percent of these residents come from Mexico. Regardless of a mounting law enforcement presence, thousands without documents pass through the country's southern borders each month—many will cross through Arizona. Of the more than six million residents who live in Arizona, approximately 360,000 are illegal. Once they successfully gain entry, a large number head further north, beyond California, Arizona, New Mexico, and Texas, in an effort to seek economic security for themselves and their families back home. Experts agree that many more illegal residents go unreported, leaving the true numbers well above any official data.

With a growing tide of hostility and increased retribution toward Hispanic immigrants, both legal and illegal, it is a perilous time. Two years have passed since Arizona governor, Jan Brewer, signed Senate Bill 1070, which requires law enforcement officers to request identification from "suspected" immigrants, and makes hiring and transporting illegal residents a crime. Like Sheriff Joe, Governor Brewer has often blamed illegal aliens for the state's economic woes and criminal activity. Many Arizonans have spoken by overwhelmingly supporting these tough-talking politicians, and along the way reignited a national debate regarding our borders and the fate of immigration. The subject of immigration is likely to remain at the political forefront for many years to come. Meanwhile, tonight, on this unassuming corner, Arizona feels disoriented and at odds with itself.

My front row ticket to this debate comes as a result of my children. As is the case with so many deeper life lessons, our children illuminate the truth. Over the course of a decade, I hired several Mexican nannies to care for my two boys, each an unlikely yet exemplary teacher and role model for both father and sons.

All came with little but gave so much. None had great career aspirations or burning desires to achieve great wealth. Although there was much at stake, each shared an understanding of life's fundamental reason for living: family. At the center of their value system: children. Their unconditional love, revered appreciation for the smallest among us, and unyielding hope through unimaginable odds demonstrated a completeness in each of these women that is worthy of emulation.

As the first, Paulina left the most enduring impression. Her enthusiasm for living, and infectious spirit were only outdone by her unending commitment and compassion for my oldest son. Carmen followed, Mormon Bible in hand, her mission to bring order to our home. Ana, ever the playmate, came and went too quickly. And finally, there was Rosa, who not only brought her love and compassion for my two boys, but her remarkable family.

While each of these women is an unlikely American heroine, all demonstrated an indisputable commitment to my children. Our time together not only made me a better man and father, but highlighted a shared value system that would overshadow any of our differences. Each woman held within her a humble desire for a more prosperous future for her family. Their journeys mirror the march of millions before and after them.

My decision to hire these women had nothing to do with a need to challenge a prevailing philosophical viewpoint, or further incite a conservative battle cry; it was simply about the well-being of children—my children. Through these women and their families, I've grown to better understand the motivations of those illegally crossing our borders, and the many commonalities they share with most Americans.

One-by-one, as reporters sign off the air and the camera lights shut down, the news crews quickly disappear. The darkness triggers the crowd to disperse. The boy, who reminds me of my own son so long ago, has since fallen asleep upon his father's shoulders. The man gently places his boy in a car seat; he's eager to return home and lay his son safely down to sleep. He gathers his other family members and drives away. For in the end, it's all about the children.

ONE

Wipe-out in Walmart

Of all places, the first real sign of trouble occurs in a Walmart bathroom. It's summer in Phoenix, early June of 1997, and hotter than hell. My legs feel like they're on fire as we enter the store, ignited by the black tar parking lot. My son and I are here to buy sandals, but he's not happy. Miguel hates wearing them and instead spots a Styrofoam glider on the end of a toy aisle. You know the ones; they're the size of a small child, made in China, and sell for five dollars.

The honeymoon is clearly over and I am in big trouble. After two years in the State of Arizona adoption system, and having overcome many objections as a single gay parent, it takes less than a week with my three-year old to come to this conclusion. As the solo pilot in this parenting gig, I am the single target of his fury. There's no disputing the fact that he's a very cute kid—all who meet him agree—but what many don't understand are his serious anger issues. Having been through a detailed screening process by the State of Arizona, I've been cautioned about this. Nonetheless, I am terrified. "All kids in the system have special needs," my social worker, Cyndi, reassures me time and time again. "Miguel is no different." When I press Cyndi for her best guess as to when things might settle down, she admits, "It's all a bit of a crap shoot."

Miguel screams without end as I race the cart forward. Although I'm new at this, I remain committed to Parenting Rule Number One: the parent is the boss, not the child. "No, you can't have that airplane," I respond with purpose. I am in charge, or at least I am making a desperate attempt to convince myself if no one else. My son strategically aims a kick at my groin and shouts, "I want it." His kicking skills are amazingly honed for such a little guy, as is his ability to make what he wants crystal clear.

In more rational moments, I remind myself that it's not unusual for adopted children to have adjustment issues. What child wouldn't want to test a new parent's commitment after being abandoned to the state welfare system? That being said, the intensity of Miguel's rage overwhelms my ability to reason clearly. Parenting books and higher education provide little guidance or comfort from this angle. Of course, returning him back within thirty days with the original receipt is not an option. Cyndi frequently reminds me of this during my many distress calls. The daily questions still surface: What was I thinking when I agreed to adopt a child with special needs? How long will the craziness last? Can I really hang on for the long term?

Somehow, during the temper tantrum, Miguel communicates another fundamental message. "I need to poop!" he screams. He's wearing Pull-ups, those diaper-like underwear that let him pee, and allow him to do his "Number 2" business without a major mess. Right now, my main responsibility is to get him positioned on the toilet and hope for the best.

I have wanted this little boy for what feels like a lifetime. I'm scared and don't want to blow this chance at parenthood. Like most new adopted parents in the state system, I'm part of what the state calls their "Fost-Adopt" program. Children are placed with a foster parent and then if all goes well over the course of one year, adoption will follow. As a result, I must gain the upper hand quickly, buckle down, and set clear boundaries. After only one week, I'm struggling to retain hope.

I rush Miguel to the bathroom, still kicking and screaming as we enter. Although Walmart has just come to Phoenix, the restroom already looks and smells like a bomb has exploded. There's something about roadside rest stops and a Walmart bathroom that give the everyday Joe a brief snapshot into prison life. As I look around and inhale, it's obvious I need to make this quick. My goal is clear: touch nothing and take shallow breaths. We choose the handicap stall by default; the other one is overflowing, with a Converse tennis shoe covered in brown goop wedged in the hole.

The stench is awful and the floor wet and grimy. Just one week earlier, I'd have done a quick about-face and left this dumping ground. Seemingly overnight, much of who I am has changed, my priorities now defined by this little boy before me.

Despite the chaos, Miguel is having no problem pooping through his rage. Later, I will come to realize that this is one of his more unusual talents. "I hate you," he yells over and over again as he goes. He is unrelenting and incredibly focused; the airplane remains his priority.

"God, this bathroom stinks!" I shout aloud, growing wearier by the second. I'm stronger than this. Or, am I? My knees begin buckling as I lean against the wall of the stall. Miguel continues kicking, screaming and crying for the toy. "I am the boss. I AM the boss. I AM THE BOSS," I chant above his considerable noise. My little boy is rapidly reducing me to some pathetic version of a Tony Robbins self-help infomercial.

My stomach tightens as the tantrum continues; I'm panicked and filled with self-doubt. I'm unwilling or possibly unable to step back and think about what Miguel is experiencing and feeling. What is he afraid of? Why is he so angry? To be candid, at this moment, I don't care. My only thought is to get us out of this hellhole. His rebellion is exhausting and all I can think about is why he won't listen. Doesn't this kid want a father? We are nose to nose when I lose it and scream, "WHAT IS YOUR PROBLEM?" In return, he hollers louder. "I hate you!" he rants.

I admit the obvious—today I shall win no awards for outstanding parenting. No doubt, there is a guardian angel, even in this Walmart bathroom, hovering and possibly even screaming at the top of her lungs, "Choose your battles wisely!" Her advice is lost over the rants of my three year old and my growing hopelessness. "I hate you!" he continues screaming, as I whimper a final, "I mean it…"

What am I NOT doing right here? Echoing through my head are the last words Cyndi told me on my front porch steps. "Two steps forward, one big step backward."

I am surprised by my own fury. Miguel's behavior is straight from the textbook. He's the one who should be angry, not me. I've spent several years preparing for this moment and now I feel like a failure. I have a lifetime ahead of me with this kid. Can it be possible that I'm already out of tricks? There must be a parental spell or two that I can cast upon him, to calm him, to achieve some level of compliance.

Fully defeated, I slide down the bathroom wall and onto the nasty floor. I look up at the fluorescent light and back at my son. Sensing he is winning, Miguel keeps up the attack. Snot running down his nose, he's not even remotely deterred.

I'm sweating, wounded, and almost down for the count. Sweating remains my primary survival mechanism in these early days of parenting. I remember little from high school science other than that our bodies must sweat to cool us from overheating. It's helping me to rebuild my physical strength to counter this persistent and diabolical behavior.

What is happening in this bathroom, on this particular day, in a Walmart, is in no way part of my original parenting plan. On a related side note, it also confirms my lifelong patronage and commitment to Target. Although I've had many dreams of fatherhood, I can place this moment in no familiar context.

Regrouping, I take a moment to find some perspective. I ask myself a few fundamental questions: "What the hell was I thinking? What exactly am I doing here? How am I going to pull off this parenting gig alone?" Perhaps the scores of friends and family who asked me these same questions before the adoption were onto something. Through forced smiles, when I first announced that I was adopting a little boy from the state system, several replied in the same way: "Such a big responsibility. Have you really thought this through?" At the time, it was so easy to reassure each of them that I had and that all would be good. I'd been successful in most things I'd put my mind to.

Lost in this moment is the utter turmoil that my son is experiencing. I'm consumed by my own sense of failure and am ignoring the motivation behind the rage that overflows from him. He's in survivor mode. So small and fragile, yet he appears invincible. He knows nothing more than to fight, push back, and protect himself. So many people have given up on him in his short life; he wears his defiance like a security blanket. Of course he'll test me. Whether I'm up for the test, or more importantly, have the courage to put myself in his shoes and can truly help him move beyond his anger, remains to be seen.

One thing becomes clear—pondering my future with Miguel will have to wait as there is something much more pressing just beyond us. I notice brown water from the clogged neighboring stall is heading our way. I quickly calculate I have less than ten seconds to get myself off the bathroom floor, grab my kid, and get out of this nightmare before we too are covered by the impending mucky river. I snap into action. I grab Miguel and reach for the toilet paper. Of course there isn't any. Now seconds away from a tidal wave, I say, "Screw it. We've got to get out of here!" Together, we pull up both Miguel's underwear and shorts and run for the exit.

There is no time to ponder what the future holds for me and my son. Gone are the hesitation and the uncertainty. I rush with him under my arms and don't stop until I reach the safety of our car. Miguel is now laughing from our great escape. I look at him and smile. He's complex and complicated and filled with so many emotions. I buckle him into his car seat. He swings his feet freely back and forth. The sight of his tennis shoes makes me laugh. In fact, I can't stop. Miguel follows suit.

As I drive away, there are two unforgettable lessons that resonate loud and clear: 1) Underwear is cheap; at the slightest hint of brown skid marks, I pledge to forever pitch any and all underwear—this includes my own. And, 2) I need help. Parenting is more than I bargained for.

TWO

Teeter Totter

My official journey to adopt a child begins several years before my meltdown in Walmart. In the State of Arizona, the process begins with a series of required parenting classes. The list of adoption requirements is long; completing an eight-week parenting class is just the first step. I find the classes insightful, yet lonely. As a gay man in a sea of married couples, I feel like a fish out of water. "Turn to your spouse and tell them when was the first time you knew that you wanted to be a parent," says Cyndi, the facilitator and assigned social worker for our group of thirty or so participants. Many of the couples in attendance are unable to conceive a child naturally; adoption is not their first choice, but now their only option. As a result, there is a tense desperation that prevails throughout the room. Apprehensively, couples turn to one another and recount their earliest desires of parenthood. Later, there is talk of sperm donors, surrogate parents and in vitro fertilization, none of which I explored. For me, adopting one of many abandoned children on this planet feels like the right direction and the only one I consider.

This is my second attempt at taking the adoption certification classes. Six months earlier, I dropped out after the first two sessions, needing to again shake the bushes of my collective soul and question my motivation and my ability to do the job alone. "It's the most important thing I've ever done," says my friend Karen, mother of two teenage boys. Over lunch, she encourages me to jump back into the adoption process. "But I'm scared shitless," I confess. "John, name me a parent who isn't," she says with a smile. "No doubt there will be crazy times, but that's what makes life interesting!"

Karen is my friend, colleague and sounding board. I have watched her and her husband nurture two boys through adolescence and teenage awkwardness, and then transition them successfully into adulthood. She is the proverbial Super Mom. A former Cub Scout leader and PTA president, she has tackled it all. She holds down a full-time job and seems to always laugh through the hardships. She sees something in me that I don't. She is there to curb my fears and anxieties, and she renews my confidence. As a result, I return to the certification classes. More than ever, I commit to my original goal and begin the adoption process again.

The classes are a combination of lecture, role playing and guest speakers, all designed to prepare us for what to expect from the children in the system. Cyndi makes the classes worthwhile and meaningful. She's funny and always honest about the road ahead. "All the kids in our system have special needs," she reminds the class over and over again. We learn many of the kids end up in the system following violent physical abuse or just plain neglect. Many more are displaced as a result of their parents' insurmountable drug addictions. Cyndi's somber tone bespeaks much of what she has witnessed firsthand from working with wounded children and the realities of the state welfare system.

With each class I teeter between confidence and cowardice. The stories from guest speakers are both heartwarming and terrifying. In our second class, an adoptive mother in her mid-forties, shares her story. "Within the first twenty-four hours my son smashed all three of our TVs and tied up his older sister," she reports. With a calm tone she describes how her son wrecked utter chaos on their otherwise peaceful household. "He was obsessed with hoarding food," she adds. "And he was good at it."

"How old is your son?" I brave the question that's on everyone's minds. "Four," she says matter-of-factly. In weeks to come, there are more speakers scheduled to scare away the weak of mind and challenge one's fortitude. Social workers remind us that disrupting placements by returning children back to the system will further damage their already fragile psyches. Testing a parent's commitment is standard fare for these kids. The classes are designed to be a realistic snapshot of what parents can expect from children in the system. Much of the content of the class is designed to teach necessary skills to help parents weather difficult transitions throughout the placement process. "You're not shopping for puppies," Cyndi lectures the group. "These are children."

Quickly, Cyndi becomes more my friend and advocate than merely my social worker. She is a mother herself, raising a teenage daughter. Like my friend Karen, she exudes life experience and shares parenting wisdom. "You are going to be a great dad," Cyndi reiterates whenever I express doubts. "One way or another, we will get it done." The stories she shares make me believe that she has moved many mountains for both parents and children.

However, her efforts have come with a price. After only two years as a social worker, I hear the weariness and discouragement in her voice. "I want to help these kids, John," she reminds me often. "That's what it's all about." This frequent mantra serves as a reminder of why she enlisted and what keeps her motivated. But the system is overwhelmed by lopsided ratios of available kids and certified parents. The local newspaper is filled with stories of abuse and neglect, and of a system that is broken due to the burgeoning Phoenix population and a long list of related societal ills that put more and more children at risk.

And yet, as a single gay man, my odds are not good. Cyndi and other social workers have been candid with me, disclosing that most all of the healthy young infants and toddlers go to married couples. Single parents are usually targeted for the older and more challenged children within the system. Still, Cyndi remains undeterred and serves as a coach, helping me navigate through a bureaucracy that places additional hurdles in front of single men, not to mention those of us who are gay. Whether mean-spirited stereotypes or outdated societal norms, being gay is a reality I must overcome if I am to be successful in adopting within the system. As a result, Cyndi counsels me to remain vague about my sexual orientation in any formal references to marital or relationship status. I've just begun the process of disclosing my sexuality openly to family and friends, so this request is not burdensome. At this point I have had no meaningful long-term relationships with men and I remain fully committed to the journey of single parenthood. Cyndi talks often about returning to teaching, but assures me this will not happen until she has found me an appropriate placement. Unequivocally, I believe her. She is earnest and committed in this pledge, which motivates and inspires me week after week.

"John, can I see you outside?" Cyndi motions me to the hallway during a long break in our fourth session. Overflowing with files in hand, she is eager to talk with me regarding a potential placement. We sit in an adjacent classroom, the two of us alone, as she lays papers over a desk. "This is highly unusual," she says. "We almost never approach parents about placements until they have finished classes and the certification process is finalized."

Paul is thirteen. By the sheer volume of documentation, I conclude that he's had a troubled past. Report after report confirms a long history of violence. Numerous placements with several families have all ended poorly. More recently, Paul's had a growing obsession with fire. As with most kids in the system, his troubles can be traced to the very beginning. He was abandoned early by his parents, both meth addicts. Several relatives stepped forward but each returned Paul like a discarded stray animal. For the last six years, he has bounced around the system from one foster family to another. He's impossible with potential siblings, unpredictable, and inappropriate with peers. No placement has lasted more than three months. Each time, Paul returns to a series of group homes in an effort to corral his anger and inappropriate behavior.

"Paul would do well with a single father who can give him lots of attention," remarks Cyndi, as if she is reading this directly from one of the adoption reports. Indeed, a group of social workers recently met to discuss Paul's fate. Cyndi has been asked by her supervisor to find a single male who would be interested in adopting him. "It sounds like there are no interested couples," I say to Cyndi frankly.

"I know you wanted a younger child, but I felt like I needed to present Paul's case," she responds. My head is spinning. I grow tense and lose focus. I have much to learn about parenting and the adoption process, yet I understand the magnitude of this moment. My answer remains monumental for both Paul and myself. Will this be my only opportunity to adopt? Several social workers have confided in me that the system makes it nearly impossible for a single man to adopt a young, reasonably healthy child. One social worker is insistent, "It just doesn't happen." Cyndi appears serious and I begin to wonder if she, too, realistically thinks this is my only opportunity. I stare at the size of the file. It's undeniable: Paul has few remaining options. Without a parent, this young teenager has no shot at childhood. Five more years in the system and he's certain to be further damaged and then, at eighteen, summarily discarded, left to fend for himself as an adult. As I review the options, I feel under the gun. Like Paul, I'm desperate. I want a chance at fatherhood as much as he needs a family.

My eyes are drawn to the survey that sits atop the pile of documents. Several months before, I'd completed a long questionnaire about the kind of child that I envisioned adopting. "Cyndi, can we read over the survey again?" I had listed my preference for a boy of any race, preferably three years of age. I had checked ADHD, Depression, Anger Issues and Previous Abuse as all acceptable conditions that I could handle as a new parent. Of course, I have no special training or skill set to manage mental illness or any of the other disorders, but that did not discourage me from checking the respective boxes. I question my own sanity as I revisit these answers.

"I don't think Paul's the one," I whisper after a long silence. Deliberately, Cindy closes the file. "John, I had to present Paul to you. I think you made the right decision." She reassures me there will be other children and that she will only present those that better meet my profile. The other couples look at us inquisitively as we re-enter the classroom. I'm distracted throughout the remainder of the class. Was Paul some kind of test to determine my wherewithal to handle children with extreme challenges? Are the social workers left with concerns about my ability to successfully parent a younger child? Will there really be another shot? Weeks later, I wake up in a sweat, with the one final question from this encounter that I had failed to ask: What's going to happen to Paul?

I have been preparing for parenthood for what seems like a lifetime. Two boys are constants in my dreams. They have no discernible faces or consistent identifiable features. We shoot baskets, play flag football, ride bikes together, and enjoy family picnics. My dreams of fatherhood include no adoring mother, wife, or partner for that matter. There is no one else but me and two boys. Why two and not one in my dreams? I cannot explain it. There have always been two and it just seems right.

My meeting with Cyndi confirms my commitment to adopt a younger child. With another week under my belt and more reflection, I place a call to Cyndi. "I don't want to miss the early years." I feel a need to further explain why I passed on Paul. It feels good to release the overwhelming feelings of guilt. I continue unrepentantly. "I want to enjoy a long list of firsts: first bike ride, first grade, first homerun, and first girlfriend."

THREE

Mine

"They're my yummy boys," jokes Cyndi. "These two are adorable, but I don't want to sugar coat it, they have some real challenges ahead of them." I hold a photo of two young boys, stepbrothers, both Hispanic. As their caseworker, Cyndi has advocated for each over the last six months. Early on, she had to make the difficult decision to separate them into different foster homes. "Their needs were too much for any one family to handle." She sounds pained by the decision. Separating them allowed each foster family to provide more individualized attention. She points to the older of the two. "He's the one…his name is Miguel." My excitement is off the charts. I am lost in the photos and do everything to focus on her words. Javier, the smaller one, shares the same mother but has a different father. Ten months older, Miguel is scheduled to go before the adoption selection panel in the next week. Several months from now and once all his paperwork is processed, Javier will face a similar panel and placement.

For almost a year I lingered in the system with little promise of a placement. Now, Cyndi will present her case as to why I am the best parent, albeit single and gay, to adopt Miguel. She will face her peers, a group of skeptical social workers, undeterred in her argument that Miguel's special needs can best be met by a single parent who can fully devote the time, attention, and energy to secure the necessary services, while ensuring a stable and loving home. As Miguel's case worker, her recommendations will carry more weight this time around. In previous attempts, this argument hasn't been well received. Other caseworkers have argued that two parent families are better equipped to address the challenges of special needs children and as a result I haven't been seriously considered for past placements. Cyndi believes underlying much of these objections is an unspoken resistance by social workers to place available children with single gay men. The system remains rife with prejudice. However, working in my favor is Miguel's age and his history of neglect and initial unruly behavior when placed in his current foster home. Undeniably, he's not an appropriate placement for those many two parent families who are looking for a healthy newborn or young toddler.

Cyndi reminds me that I will be positioned against two other families. Each "staffing," as such meetings are known within the system, always includes three families, but only one is selected. Out of step with protocol, she divulges that the other two families under consideration are both married couples with children. They will also have a caseworker present who will make a persuasive argument for why it will take two parents (a man and a woman) to successfully raise Miguel. In representing both me and Miguel, Cyndi must walk a fine line in capturing what's in Miguel's best interest. This will demand a Herculean argument on Cyndi's part in her effort to persuade her critics to set aside stereotypes. "Don't forget, even if the committee picks you, you still have major hurdles to jump through," she advises as she hands me five additional photos of Miguel from the file. She begins to recap the long "Fost-Adopt" program which I will need to successfully complete.

From what I gather from Cyndi in the upcoming weeks, if all goes well with the selection committee there will be several initial meetings with Miguel to determine if the two of us are indeed a good match. Thereafter, I will serve as Miguel's foster parent for one year, which allows for a formal courtship to further validate the pairing. During this time, a series of state welfare workers will regularly visit our home to evaluate and determine if I am an acceptable parent. Then, and only then, may I apply for adoption.

As she continues with further details, I am fully distracted and a million miles away. As I shuffle between photos, I can't take my eyes off Miguel. He is adorable. At three, he sits alone on a tile floor in a small cramped room of his foster home. He's all smiles. He plays with wooden blocks and his large dimples radiate. In each photo, he looks directly into the camera and appears healthy and satisfied. He's mesmerizing. "Can this finally be the one?" I dare ask.

Four days pass before Cyndi calls; she's so excited she can barely speak. "You're it! You're it!" She says that I have been selected over the two other couples. Ever-persuasive, Cyndi prevailed over numerous objections. In doing so, she kept an earlier pledge for which I will be eternally indebted. Only later am I privy to the concerns raised by the panel about a gay, single dad adopting a young boy.

Suddenly, I will be given my shot and I am catapulted into a new reality. Prior to this phone call, there's been little at risk and even less at stake. Over the last twelve months, I have been stalled in my safe and secure world. Throwing in the towel remained an option. However, Cyndi's call has changed my life forever. Now I'm no longer on deck, but at bat. Equally excited and terrified, I remain silent through Cyndi's detailed description of next steps. In less than a week, I will meet Miguel for the first time. Parenting books and classroom training will be out the window in exchange for a small boy whom I will soon call son. "John, did you hear me? Did you hear me, John? You're it!" After the awkward silence I ask, "What if he doesn't like me?"

Cyndi acts quickly before the adoption committee second-guesses their decision or her prospective parent loses his courage. She arranges for me to meet Miguel and his foster mother. The visit is intended to be short – a brief opportunity to meet one another and serve as a time to test the waters.

Prior to our meeting, I revisit the pictures of the little boy. I carry them with me and look at them often. I'm both excited and conflicted. He looks sweet and kind and filled with unlimited energy. However, I know from Cyndi's briefing that Miguel has struggled in his adjustment. Both brothers have a history of uncontrolled rage when they don't get their way. With other children, they fight often. Miguel, in particular, breaks things. It's this unpredictability that leads Ramona, the boys' foster mother, to request that Javier be placed elsewhere. She feels she'll have more success in handling Miguel alone. She makes this difficult decision knowing she must also look after the welfare of her three other foster children. Regardless of this background, I am beside myself with excitement to meet him. Miguel's brown eyes and unending smile, with the two perfect dimples, unlock untapped emotions within me. He deserves a break in life, not to mention a permanent home.

As I press Cyndi for more details on his past, she gives me Miguel's entire file, both the good and the bad. To her credit and against all regulations, she wants me to fully understand what I am taking on and encourages me to read everything. I am both intrigued and repulsed by the large accordion file. Part of me wants to discount the data before me and give Miguel a fresh start. However, a louder and more practical voice calls me back to the many documents within the file, which attempt to explain Miguel and his difficult start. Hundreds of pages capture the extensive abandonment and neglect. Before his current placement, Miguel lived a nomadic life, left with anyone who would care for him. Reports chronicle his drug exposure at birth, lack of parental love, and initial bonding. Other documentation identifies his mother's drug habit and a cycle of abuse that stretches for generations. Miguel's foster mother, Ramona, is the first to offer unconditional love and stability in his short life. Pragmatically, I conclude the key to this boy rests somewhere amongst the many pages scattered on my kitchen counter and the six photos that now live permanently in my back pocket.

I gather the documents and put them back in the folder, placing the large file out of sight. I decide I cannot further cloud the process—I must meet Miguel before I come to any conclusions. I owe him this much. Why should he be judged and burdened by a dysfunctional past that he had no control over? My mind teeters between the mesmerizing photos of an angelic three year-old and the stark reality of the documentation of abuse and neglect. In the end, my emotions win out over any empirical data and I cast aside the large file.

I arrive twenty minutes early and find myself circling the neighborhood several times to burn both time and anxiety. The block is a collection of small ranch style homes built in the sixties, with single open carports. It's April and the grass is green, however the homes look overgrown and tired with the exception of the large grapefruit trees that overflow with flowering buds. The trees, no doubt, are survivors of an earlier citrus grove on this land. The many fragrant flowers attach to the drooping branches like Christmas ornaments, which gives this modest neighborhood hope. Ranchero music blasts from somewhere in the distance. Ramona lives just blocks away from Desert Samaritan Hospital in Mesa, where Miguel was born. Based on their last known address, his birth mother and maternal grandparents appear to live very near this neglected neighborhood.

A tiny boy dressed in baggy green shorts and a striped shirt stands alone at the end of the driveway. I am not completely certain I know who I'm looking at. The boy's hair is long and his face is lost somewhere behind dangling bangs. Nervously, I double check to ensure that I'm at the intended address. He looks alone and very different from the pictures that I have dissected over the last week. "Are you Miguel?" I ask as I approach. He clutches a picture of a red dog that he's drawn with crayons for this special occasion. He extends his tiny arm, handing over his prized drawing, and says, "here." He is shy and timid and with good reason – I must appear in giant proportion to his teacup-size. "Thanks for the picture, I really like it," I tell him in a calm voice, hoping not to scare him. I take his small hand in mine and we walk up to the house.

There, at the front door, I meet Ramona. She is all smiles as she sees the two of us holding hands. Ramona is a short and sturdy Hispanic woman; her long grey hair is pulled into a ponytail that stretches partway down her back. She's in her mid-sixties and wears a faded cotton dress. The children call her *Abuela*, grandmother, in Spanish. She's lively, warm, and friendly from our initial greeting. I sense she's worked hard throughout her life. We hug briefly and then she ushers me inside. Her home is tiny but tidy. The interior walls are white painted brick and the floors are tiled throughout. The ceiling sits low to my head. She points, directing me to sit in the small family room. There are two worn black overstuffed leather loveseats that leave space for little else. I recognize this room from the photos. A box of building blocks sits near a small children's play table. "These are the blocks that Miguel was playing with in the pictures," I say nervously as I pull out the photos from my back pocket, as if I must convince her. A seasoned parent, Ramona talks slowly and calmly, while thoughtfully looking over the photos. "He loves to build," she says. Miguel is glued to her side. For nine months he has lived with her, longer than anyone else in his short life. She is the closest thing to a mother that he has experienced.

We sit on opposite loveseats and our conversation begins to naturally unfold. "He can spend hours building." A veteran of motherhood, she sounds wise and noble. She exudes a confidence that only comes from years of parenting. She tells me of the many foster children she has nurtured over the last decade in addition to raising her own children. Ramona plays an active role with several granddaughters who live nearby, as well as the four foster children now living with her. She works as a teacher's aide in a public school just down the street, assisting young kids who are learning English as a second language. "God has called me to care for children," she says. "It's what I do."

Miguel is nearly attached to Ramona, his body bent over and head resting on her lap. She gently combs his long hair with her fingers. He's quiet throughout our conversation. "He is ready," she continues, as she gently strokes her hand across his face. Clearly, he finds comfort from the gentle and repetitive motion. "He needs someone to love him and give him a new life full of opportunities." At this moment, Miguel looks completely content and free of his tumultuous past. Ramona's English is nearly flawless, but there remains a slight accent, indicating her likely start in Mexico many years before. She clarifies her foster children come from different ethnic backgrounds and with many different languages. So for the most part she speaks English, although she says she finds herself slipping in and out of Spanish throughout the day. She adds that Miguel's primary language was Spanish; however, he now speaks English fluently. "You have no wife?" she asks, somewhat randomly. It's hard to read her but she remains friendly. "No, it's just me," I say elusively.

Edgar and Jimmy come running into the small family room from the hallway, both eager to steal the attention away from their foster brother. Miguel does not move but his eyes briefly dart towards them as a warning to keep their distance. He remains transfixed on me. His stare explicitly marks his territory and the boys stop in their tracks. Cyndi has given me a heads-up that Edgar has been biting Miguel over the last two months. As a result, she is eager to transition him soon into a permanent placement.

"Will you be my dad?" Edgar asks abruptly. Like Miguel, he is three years-old and Hispanic, but considerably shorter. He doesn't smile easily but is desperate for attention. Edgar lunges toward me and hugs me longer than I am comfortable; I have to literally pull him from me. Jimmy, full of smiles, is four, white, and thin to the bone. He holds a football under one arm and reaches with his free hand and shakes from a distance. He is an outgoing and funny kid, with freckles on his nose and cheeks. Both Jimmy and Edgar stand at attention in front of me as if auditioning. I look over at Miguel who has a scowl on his face. My heart aches for all of them.

"Do you guys like to play football?" I ask. "What a great idea," Ramona says as she stands up to hold the screen door open. The boys quickly pile out the front door. She smiles at me and appears excited at the prospect of a man in the house—or if nothing else, relieved at the prospect of the boys burning off excess energy. We play for the next thirty minutes, sweating from the heat, and drink several times from the garden hose to cool down. Miguel and I are a team against Jimmy and Edgar. Touch football quickly turns to tackle. All three boys laugh as I pile one on top of the other. Soon after, Ramona and Liliana bring out lemonade in a plastic Kool-Aid pitcher. Liliana is the remaining foster child. She's sweet and soft-spoken, and looks about seven. Hispanic, she is skinny with long dark straight brown hair and lanky legs. "Want some?" she asks simply, as she holds the tray out before me. I tower over Ramona and the four children and feel colossal. They look up as if they are staring well beyond my face and into the open sky above.

"Mine," Miguel says to Edgar and Jimmy later as they each try to sit on my lap. Categorically, Miguel stakes his claim. We sit in the shady grass under the canopy of the large overgrown grapefruit tree. Miguel has made it clear that I am here to see him. I wonder who else has come to visit this household and under what pretense. At such a young age, they seemingly understand they must vie for attention to gain their exit. Each appears ready and willing to claim their ticket, wanting once and for all to have a permanent home. Based on their instinctive territorial actions, they know the significance of this visit. At some level, I'd rather not know why.

"How do you guys like school?" I ask them about their daily routines at daycare. Fearing the other boys may take his place, Miguel remains glued to my lap. They all agree they like their preschool but talk of hating a boy named Raul who is a bully and lives several houses away. "We don't like him," Miguel tells me. "He is not allowed to come over anymore," says Jimmy. "I like Legos," Miguel says impulsively, changing the subject as he runs back into the house. In his absence, the two boys know better than to take his place. He brings me a small sturdy house he has made of colorful Lego blocks, and hands it to me as he secures himself firmly back in my lap. His dimples light up and he's excited and proud. "Wow, you are a good builder," I whisper in his ear. "You are such a smart boy."

My visit is short but has served its purpose. I've made a connection. As the boys and I talk under the tree, I imagine Miguel's future, which will be vastly different from this vantage point. His new world will be filled with endless opportunities beyond this modest neighborhood. If all goes well, it will soon be my primary responsibility to guide him down this path. The impending charge humbles and terrifies me.

"Can we come to your house?" asks Edgar through the car window. All three are clamoring with excitement and all are equally adorable. They're eager to climb in my backseat and appear content with never returning. Part of me wants to unlock the back door and take all three. Ramona grabs each of the boys' hands and pulls them back from my car as I drive away.

The next day, I purchase a car seat and an oversized blue bouncy ball at Target. The following weekend, I meet Miguel's court appointed legal advocate in front of a large train engine that anchors a Mesa city park not far from Ramona's house. Cyndi has warned me that this woman, as a representative of the courts, has the power to block my adoption if she feels like we're not a good match. "As his advocate, her primary welfare is that of Miguel," Cyndi says, reminding me of what's at stake. "Be on your best behavior and turn on some of that magic."

As the three of us gather in front of the huge rusting locomotive, I feel self-conscious as I engage Miguel in small talk. The advocate, a young woman, quickly volunteers that she's a mother of two girls. She's friendly and appears genuine as we talk about where we grew up. Our conversation is short, but positive and comes easy. At some point, she begins taking notes as I resume talking with Miguel. Soon, the two of us are engulfed in play and I forget her watchful eyes. He insists that I chase him around the play set, and using the big blue ball, we play tag. He laughs when it bounces off his head. He's happy. "He's an amazing kid," I say in between drinks from the water fountain. "The two of you look like you are hitting it off nicely," Miguel's advocate says. "You guys will do well together."

Her comments are a relief and serve as a generous gift to an apprehensive father-in-training. We sit and talk while watching Miguel play on the monkey bars. He's fearless as he climbs and joins several other children. When it's time to go, Miguel plants himself at the top of the structure and refuses to come down. He screams, and as I climb to retrieve him, he grabs my neck tightly. He is frantic and struggles as his advocate attempts to place him in the car seat, clearly not wanting to return to his foster home. "I want him," he says over and over, uncertain what to call me. Desperation rings out in his voice as if I am forever abandoning him. "I want him," he continues screaming through the open car window as the two pull away from the parking lot.

At lunch the next day with my friend Karen, I recap the two visits with Miguel. "Does he seem like he's the one?" she asks. "Did you know it from the minute you saw him?" Although I have asked these same questions, I struggle to answer. I have read about birth mothers who have an immediate bond with their newborns as they are placed in their arms. There is no doubt with each visit that my feelings grow stronger and stronger for Miguel, but understanding this is a forever commitment leaves me questioning if he's really the one.

A week later, Cyndi calls and indicates everything is going well and that she's arranged for a sleepover. The process feels like we're suddenly in high gear. Miguel swims for the first time in my back-yard pool and immediately takes to the water. "Catch me, catch me, catch me," he screams but jumps in before he can get the last words out. He surfaces with a terrified expression and a mouthful of water. He applies a death grip to my neck, a familiar occupational hazard that I remember from years before as a teenager, when I taught swim lessons to children.

Miguel's disposition is sweet; his behavior is angelic and above all he appears grateful for every minute we are together. I see no signs of a troubled past in our initial gatherings. This helps push the doubts aside. At these times, I can easily block out the large accordion file I have tucked firmly away in the kitchen cabinet. Since meeting Miguel, I've not ventured back to it. Honeymoon period or not, I see unlimited potential in this boy before me.

We sit on the carpet in what is to be Miguel's bedroom. I've moved my desk and computer to the third bedroom in anticipation of his arrival. There's nothing in the room but a few boxes stacked along one wall and a brown sleeping bag and pillow on the carpet. There are a handful of games and puzzles that sit on the shelves in the otherwise empty closet. We've just returned from picking out Miguel's new bed and Superman sheets. Cyndi has encouraged this joint shopping trip to instill a sense of empowerment and belonging. He should be exhausted from shopping and our swim, but he's not. Together, we build Lego blocks. He is intent on constructing a fort. Ramona, his foster mother, is right—he can build for hours on end. Unbeknownst to me, my mom has let herself in through the front door. She watches the two of us for some time before Miguel looks up and spots her. "I made this," he says to her proudly, unaware of her significance. "Miguel, this is your new grandma," I say to him. Until now, the two haven't met. Without direction, he gets up and gives her a hug. "Nice to meet you," my mom bends over and hugs him tight. "You are such a good builder," she says. He goes back to his blocks as the two of us walk down the hall. "He is a little angel boy," she says nearly tearing up. She's overcome with emotion from her brief encounter with her newest grandchild.

One week later, Miguel is refusing to get out of his car seat. "No, no, no, no...." he grabs tightly as I attempt to pry him free. I have picked him up from his foster home for the day. My entire family has gathered at our annual Memorial Day barbeque. We sit idle in front of my parents' home as the temperature soars well over one-hundred degrees. From the backyard swimming pool, Miguel hears laughing and screams from his future cousins. He is overwhelmed at the thought of seeing so many new faces. Just beyond the block fence he must sense the eagerness of his four cousins. "Miguel, Grandma has a big pool in her backyard. Don't you want to go swimming?" I ask, attempting to distract him from his fears. "No, no, no..." he continues as I maneuver the seatbelt over his head. Our wrestling match becomes a stalemate when he accidentally kicks me in the eye with his tennis shoe. All four doors wide-open, I leave him in the boiling car as I flag my mom down in the kitchen for assistance. "Mom, he won't get out," I say. "He must be terrified of meeting everyone," she says instinctively. She grabs a snack pack of Oreo cookies, puts on a smile, and says, "Let me give it a try."

Within minutes, Miguel and his grandma walk hand-in-hand through the front door. "Daddy, look who's here?" my mom sings out cheerfully. Miguel's hair is matted and wet from the broiling car. Now happy, he reaches for my hand and eats cookies.

As we step outside, Miguel squeezes my hand harder and leans against me. He remains silent and looks away from all the strange faces. Every ounce of him wants to jump into the pool but he fights the inclination as he's taken back by the rowdy group of children. "Hi Miguel," sing out the group of his new cousins. "We've been waiting for you. Do you like to swim?" They are eager for him to play. Miguel keeps his head down and refuses to acknowledge them. All the while, the water calls his name. It takes all his strength not to dive into the cool water. He wills himself to stay grounded and away from the unfamiliar faces.

We keep our visit short but Miguel leaves knowing he has an extended family that is eager to love him. Before we pull out, my dad comes running to the car with a small toolbox that he has pulled together, with a hammer, screws, nails, pieces of small wood, and several screwdrivers. "I understand we have a builder in the family," my dad says, unable to contain his excitement as he hands Miguel the small blue metal box. "I have lots of projects planned for the two of us when you come back to visit your grandpa." Miguel quickly spreads the contents across the backseat.

As we drive away, I remain distracted by the car seat in which Miguel is now securely fastened. I revisit it regularly in my rear-view mirror, needing to confirm whether it is occupied or not. At times I'm obsessed by it. The seat is almost surreal. It signifies a reality which for so long was just a dream. Driving home, Miguel has quickly fallen asleep, hugging his new hammer. His other new tools lay everywhere. It's quiet in the car with the exception of the air conditioner pumping cold air throughout the vents. I'm taken back by the simplicity of the moment. My little boy is precious and safe, with a slight smile on his sleeping face. Once and for all I realize I can do this. This is meant to be and there's no turning back. Once and for all, I am this little boy's father.

"It's time John." Cyndi confirms the finality of it all in an early morning phone call on a Wednesday. It's June 4, 1997 and it has come down to one final drive to the modest Mesa subdivision, near the hospital, just two months after we first met. I am to pick up Miguel on Friday afternoon, leave with one stuffed animal and one little boy. There is nothing left but to start our new life together.

Miguel is happy and runs up to hug me. "He's here, he's here," he yells to Ramona and the other children. He is anxious to leave and immediately heads to the car, pulling at my hand. It seems like years have passed since I first spotted this boy with his shaggy hair standing alone at the end of the driveway. I carry him back to the house to give Ramona a final hug. She cries, kissing him on both cheeks. She hands me a small plastic shopping bag with the one stuffed animal. She's done her job well and prepared yet another wounded child for transition. After loving Miguel so fully, she is valiant in her selflessness as she now hands him over with no strings attached. She's got nothing but best wishes for the two of us. I couldn't do the same. I would not have the wherewithal to cut this child free. Our courtship period has softened me and I begin to cry. "You call me with any questions," she says, pulling me aside. "And, you love him. More than anything else—love him."

Miguel hops into his car seat. I no longer struggle to strap him in. He fits like a glove. It's all happened so quickly and now feels right. As I pull forward and down the street, Miguel's dimples shine from the rearview mirror. He has no interest in turning around – no desire to look back at the life he leaves behind. Further back, I notice Edgar has darted from the house and is running behind the car, crying, finally collapsing to the street in hysterics. Ramona trails closely behind.

FOUR

Adiós Amigo

A group of soccer moms from the neighborhood looks like they've just crashed their minivans when I first tell them that I've placed an ad in the newspaper to find a nanny. We're gathered at the neighborhood grade school. Miguel and I have been a team for just a few weeks now, and fitting into this club of moms is going to take some getting used to.

We're watching our kids, who range in age from three to five, weave through little red cones as part of the peewee soccer league that meets every Sunday afternoon. Miguel is in the middle of the pack, and laughing with several other children as they run by us. As the only Hispanic kid here, he's easy to pick out. The team is led by a stocky, red-headed female soccer coach, who likely played at the collegiate level. Kicking the ball far ahead of the heavily distracted army of pencil-sized figurines, she barks out orders as she might to a group of high school freshmen, in hopes of keeping them on task.

"You're going to trust your son with some stranger?" asks the neurotic mother who lives around the corner from us, her judgment unmistakable. Several days earlier, she was spitting in my face in a huff because her son was hurt playing kickball in our front yard. Since then, she's declared her two boys are no longer allowed to play with Miguel. The "Fitness Fanatic" soon jumps on the bandwagon and adds, "There are a lot of stranger dangers out there! Don't you worry about that?"

The ad I placed seems straightforward:

> *Single dad, seeking loving, caring nanny for three year-old boy. Spanish speaking preferred; references and transportation a must.*

A friend from work has had good luck more than once finding Spanish-speaking babysitters, by placing a similar ad in the "Domestic" section of the local newspaper. She doesn't have the required $2,500 finder's fee to pay an agency. As it is, she and her husband will struggle to pay for in-home care but both feel strongly that they want their children at home until they're ready for preschool.

Based on my friend's experiences, I'm convinced I too want a Spanish-speaking babysitter who can teach Miguel a second language at an early age. I want a caretaker who looks like he does and can provide a connection to his culture that he'll otherwise struggle to find in our neighborhood. It's no secret that Hispanics will be the majority population in the not-so-distant future; this is true especially in the Southwest. My friend and her husband, who is English, believe mastering Spanish will be a definite advantage for their children as they grow up, and I agree. They're not threatened by the language, but rather talk about it as another positive aspect of living in Arizona. Situated adjacent to Mexico, our lives and fundamental reference points are inherently connected to a Hispanic culture that long predated any white settlement of the area. Our language, food, architecture, clothing, music, and art are intertwined. From this broader perspective, I don't have a need to stake out territorial boundaries or draw lines in the sand.

A Spanish-speaking nanny will definitely be an asset. If she happens to only speak Spanish, all-the-better. Total immersion will assure Miguel's former fluency returns that much quicker. As a result, I'm eager to get the search process underway. Hitting the ground running with an extra set of hands cooking and cleaning will be a big help as well. And Miguel will welcome the variety. Whether it is spaghetti or barbecued chicken, he's already grown tired of my usual side dishes of beans and watermelon that accompany most of the meals I serve up.

My friend confirms that as long as I'm willing to weed through a number of "crazy" applicants and check out references, good candidates will surface. Her current nanny has bonded quickly with her two small children. In passing, she mentions that the woman is in the country illegally; she came to the U.S. on a travel visa more than two years ago and never left. But she is a gentle and sweet caretaker, and fully committed to the well-being of the children. My friend sings her praises with saint-like reverence. "I wish I had her patience," she says glowingly.

Others struggle with my decision to hire a nanny from Mexico, who may also be here without documents. While working out in the gym with me, a friend asks, "What if your nanny has a son who's a gangbanger?" I laugh at the randomness of his question. "You mean, kind of like, if Alice from *The Brady Bunch* were to have a rogue child with nasty tattoos all over his body?" Clearly worried that I'm not taking his warnings seriously, he adds, "No, I mean, what if she's a drug dealer?"

Having not grown up in Phoenix, my friend has had limited exposure to the scores of productive undocumented residents and the vibrant economy that supports them. His fears of drugs and gangs are fueled by conservative talk radio hosts, who project a fabricated reality separate from the experience of the majority of alien residents who are hard-working and only want for a better life. I have several neighbors and friends who have come to Phoenix as new transplants and now somehow want to claim sole ownership of the state. The newest among them are some of the most strident. Ideally, they would handpick all new arrivals and interview prospective neighbors, a new twist on the iconic Western Sheriff charged with rooting out the bad guys. Listening to their discussions of who is "good" and who is "bad" can be disconcerting on so many levels.

For those who are raised in the Southwest, there is an innate understanding that many of the hardest working men and women among us labor illegally in restaurants, resorts, construction sites, office buildings, and landscaping crews, and do much of the work others will not. Millions of illegal residents are working in this country and being paid under the table. This creates a large and dynamic underground economy. These workers choose to come to this country for one overriding reason: to seek a more prosperous life for themselves and their families. Drugs and gangs are no more a reality in their lives than the many Americans who cast stones upon them.

As a kid, I never questioned why illegal immigrants came to this country. Thanks to my parents, I understood. Our family enjoyed camping trips in the rugged and remote mountains of Northern Arizona, but also vacationed along the beaches of Mexico. These getaways didn't take place in high-rise hotels in Acapulco or Puerto Vallarta; rather, we camped on beaches in tents. Later, when modest blue collar prosperity came to our family, a small travel trailer followed, which allowed for more creature comforts. Our destination was almost always the same: Puerto Penasco—Rocky Point, as it's known to Arizonans. More than forty years ago, traveling in our maroon '68 Chevy station wagon, Rocky Point was a sleepy fishing village, five hours drive from Phoenix. Poverty defined my earliest memories of Mexico. It was everywhere. Wealth was securely tucked behind a few gated beachside American communities. We stayed outside these fortresses in a trailer park called Playa del Oro (Beach of Gold). Coin operated showers and a shared indoor toilet were the extent of the amenities; the beach remained the unmistakable calling card. For those traveling from Tucson and Phoenix, Rocky Point was an extension of the United States. Cursory inspections took place by border guards, but legitimate fears of drug lords and roadside violence were non-existent.

When traveling to Mexico, my dad had a routine. Each visit included stops to the Mexican bakery just off the main drag of town, as well as the local Coke distributor. These core supplies would supplement the food packed snugly in a large cooler. Another high-light was the fish market on the pier, where my parents made an effort to speak the language when negotiating with local fisher-men for their freshest seafood and largest shrimp. Doing so, my parents developed an honest respect for the people of Rocky Point. They saw first-hand how difficult life was for the average Mexican, and yet how warm and generous they were to the many American visitors, especially their children. My parents could relate to their struggles and focus on family. Rocky Point had little of the com-mercialization and pretense that existed along well-known border towns like Tijuana or the large swanky vacation destinations like Puerto Vallarta. This humble town was a more accurate snapshot of the stunning poverty that most Mexican families endured.

While my brothers and I played in the ocean with boogie boards and went spear-fishing in the coral during low tide, the Mexican children toiled in the sun alongside their parents, selling souvenirs to the Americans camped along the beach. We were unmistakable with our pale skin slathered with zinc oxide, the same white cream worn by lifeguards. The Mexicans sold us what they could: colorful traditional serapes and blankets, knick-knacks, jewelry, toys, fire-works, and Chiclets. The Mexican men and boys dressed in long pants and shirts and black dress shoes, sledged through the sand, their backs weary with wares. The parents doggedly pointed and directed their children to approach everyone along the beach.

My parents were deeply moved by the plight of these children, whose daily struggles to survive in Mexico never went unnoticed. A cloud of despair seemingly stalled over this small piece of the world, unchanged from visit to visit. "What do you think your lives would be like if you were born in Mexico?" My dad would ask as we drove by one of the many tarpaper homes, not wanting to miss one of life's teachable moments, and hoping to instill some small kernel of compassion.

Returning from Mexico one summer, I met a boy at the bor-der who was selling gum. He and his two younger brothers ap-proached each car of Americans as they waited to pass into the

U.S. This image of young venders is forever locked in my memory. The line of cars was longest on Sunday afternoons, as sunburned Americans impatiently waited for Mexican officials to inspect their vehicles. The boy walked alongside our station wagon as we slowly inched forward. Our conversation was short but memorable and his English was good. We quickly found out that we were both the same age. He, the oldest of three children—I, the youngest. We both played baseball and loved to swim. He pointed to his two younger brothers several rows over from us, who were working the unfriendly crowd of American tourists, many refusing to open their car windows. This was their daily routine, and as a result, the boys appeared undaunted by rejection.

At the last minute, I slipped him what little change I had, some gesture of friendship or guilt. In return, he offered me a box of Chiclets. *"No, no Gracias. Adiós Amigo!"* I said awkwardly—surprising myself for spitting out some small response in Spanish.

As the Mexican border guards questioned my dad, I stared back at the three brothers. The youngest approached a pick-up truck with a big, blue camper anchored upon it. The driver, who showed no interest in the boy or the gum, flicked a cigarette butt at him as he rolled up his window.

FIVE

Try Her - You'll Like Her!

The coffee cup comes from nowhere. Sitting on a stool at the kitchen counter eating his lunch, Miguel whips it at me with a quick clip. I duck as it crashes against the refrigerator and smashes to the ground. He throws another.

"Miguel, we're not going swimming until you take a nap," I say again. He has successfully stretched his lunchtime to more than thirty minutes to avoid this moment, and we're at a familiar and volatile crossroads. "No," he says over and over again. He's now standing upright on the kitchen counter, pulling plates out of cabinets and slamming them one at a time on the floor. "Don't you…" I say as I attempt to grab him, but not before he lobs one final dish at me. It misses my head and crashes against the refrigerator. I take him from the counter kicking and screaming, and head to his room, walking atop a mosaic of broken glass. "Five minutes of time out and then it is naptime," I yell over his screams. It's official: the asylum is again out of control.

Following the textbook, I place Miguel in the corner of his room, without toys or other distractions. This has become a familiar spot. He must stay here for five minutes; the parenting books are all quite clear on this. I attempt to communicate through his rage that his outburst is unacceptable and I shut his door. He is instantly up and throwing his toys around the room. He pulls the sheets out from under his mattress, while hollering as loud as he is able. His screams sound primitive – they seem to come from some dark recess within. I hear the dresser tumble, but this time I choose not to go in and redirect him back to the designated corner. I've done this dozens of times in the past month with little success. Screw the parent manuals and self-help books. Today, I'm not moving from this wall.

This is more about bravado, I convince myself. He wants me to react, or better yet overreact; he's taunting me back into battle. He exalts when pulling me into his darkness. I won't go—not today. So I wait. Just outside his room, I lean against the wall. I breathe deeply and feel alone. I know this spot better than any other in the house: the cobweb above the door molding; the scratch on the top corner of the hall closet door; the light fixture missing a bulb; the chocolate syrup stain on the beige carpet just in front of my feet. It's dark here and cool. This time, I will wait it out.

How did we get here? Clearly the honeymoon is over, but when did we arrive in hell? The change came swiftly but it's nonetheless confounding. My son seemingly can turn evil on and off on a dime. One moment he can be sweet and affectionate, and then oppositional, apparently fighting for his right to do what he wants, when he wants, for as long as he wants. Coming from such a small child, it would frighten the best of parents, not to mention a new single father who has been masquerading as one prepared and capable.

Unable to wait any longer, I push the door open to find Miguel punching his bedroom window, and attempting with all his will to shatter the pane. He cracks it; one more swing and the large window will surely buckle. His tiny fist outstretched, Miguel turns and cries, fearful of his own rage. His mattress lies in the middle of the floor, his clothes and toys everywhere. The room looks like a war zone. I place him back in the dedicated timeout corner. He's exhausted, uncharacteristically so, and stays put. I struggle to find compassion over the fear and anger, which easily win out. I'm furious at this child and his unfailing defiance. Where is the little boy who cried every time I left him behind at his foster home? What happened to the toddler with the cute dimples and the loving hug? Fear whirls through my veins but I attempt to block it as terror successfully reaches my brain.

I feel defenseless and have nothing that resembles an effective game plan. Even with the adoption classes, I have few concrete tactics to address our daily struggles. Day-to-day living is discouraging, and at times I want nothing more than to throw in the towel, pack him up, drop him off at my social worker's cubicle, and say, "You deal with him." After little more than a month, the optimism is all but gone. During these times, I lock myself in the bathroom to escape his fury and anger. Locked safely behind the door, I cry. Not loudly, because I don't want him to know he has won the battle.

I have yet to take Ramona up on her offer, but today, with my fear finally overriding my pride, I have no other choice but to call Miguel's foster mother. I convince myself it's been a victory to have waited this long. I desperately need someone who can validate the anger and rage. She's one of the few who has seen it and must have some insights; some small nuggets of wisdom into who this boy is and how to speak to his needs. With all the children she's raised over the years, certainly she'll have answers.

"He broke a window when he lived with me too," Ramona confesses when I call. She explains that she opted not to report the incident to Miguel's case worker because she didn't want them to take him away. She believes in Miguel. "You're the right one for him," she continues, discounting my lack of confidence. She explains that she told Cyndi Miguel needed a two parent family, but once she saw me with him she knew we were the right match. "What was it that you saw in me?" I ask. "I saw love," she says kindly. "What you need now is patience."

"What do I do with his anger?" I ask. "You need to love him," she repeats simply. "There are no easy solutions with this child." She replays her own battles with my son, who prides himself on his endurance and need for control in the heat of battle. "John, he's strong-willed; you need to find another way. Make him feel like he's the boss."

Ramona believes that Miguel tries to control what little he can as a result of never bonding soon after birth. He learned to protect and look after himself to survive. She's filled with wise and priceless insight and I continually thank her throughout our conversation. At the end of the call, we promise to stay in touch. In the meantime, Miguel has fallen asleep. Later on, we swim in an effort to cleanse away the earlier battle. For both father and son, these swims serve as a respite from daily combat.

I am more convinced than ever that I need help, but who will be willing? The task at hand is no small undertaking. Miguel's emotional issues are real and his behavior scary. Whoever signs on board will have their hands full, and will need to be ready to face firestorms. With just a few weeks left before I return to work, I'm down to the wire and need to find a nanny. I've had several phone interviews with women who lack the qualifications to care for children, and a few who sound downright peculiar. I've arranged a meeting with a woman who is described by her aunt as "loving and fun with children." I need fun back in my life; I'm anxious and curious. I agree to first meet at the aunt's house.

As we enter, Paulina fills the kitchen doorway. At 300-plus pounds, she's indeed large; big by every stretch of the imagination. Dressed in an oversized t-shirt and full cotton skirt, her size is immediately appealing as my three year-old is lost in her embrace.

Paulina lives with her Aunt Irma in an old, Spanish adobe style home in a historic district called Willo in downtown Phoenix. Ten years later, this home will be worth fourfold as yuppies look to revitalize the area. It's July 1997 and for now the house is nothing more than modest and desperately in need of renovation.

From the get-go, Paulina is the one. She captivates Miguel, who loves the opportunity to sit on the ground and play with her and Barbie, Paulina's toy poodle. She wastes no time taking Pepe, the parrot, from his cage in the small kitchen, and has him repeat "Miguel" over and over. Paulina, Pepe, Barbie, and Miguel are fully engaged within the first five minutes of our arrival. Paulina speaks in Spanish, and to my surprise, Miguel understands most every word.

As I watch this woman engage my son, I'm taken by her playful manner. Facing him on the tile floor, eye to eye, she talks easily and is animated. She seems to know just what to say to keep Miguel engaged. "*Te gustan los animales?*" She asks my son if he likes animals. What little boy doesn't? Miguel now has Barbie the poodle on his lap and Pepe the parrot perched on his shoulder. Despite her large size, Paulina has an ease and confidence about her that makes her even more intriguing and inviting.

Irma is gracious but eager to lock down a firm employment commitment. We tour her small, tidy two-bedroom home. It's dark and warm—the swamp cooler rattles away in each of the postage-stamp sized rooms. Decades ago, the adobe walls had been painted a brilliant white, but now it's peeling from much of the ceiling, a result of condensation. Paulina and her husband Sergio's belongings are overflowing from the small secondary bedroom with the king-size bed. There's barely room to walk so I peer in from the safety of the doorway.

Irma invites me to sit with Paulina on a small loveseat. The scene quickly turns comical as the two of us try to wedge ourselves into it. Embarrassed, Irma waves me to the kitchen, where she waits for me behind the refrigerator. There, she whispers somewhat desperately in my ear: "Paulina is a big, big girl, but she has a good heart. You'll like her. I know you'll like her." Paulina appears unfazed by her large girth, and for me, her size is irrelevant. What genuinely excites me about her is her uninhibited spirit and the unbridled affection she directs at my child. Irma and I are silent for a few long seconds as I smile awkwardly and slip by her with a quick, "Gracias" as I head back to Paulina, who waits in the living room.

Paulina and I relay an unspoken message, communicated solely through our eye contact and quick smiles, an acknowledgement of Irma's private conversation. Paulina is unfazed by the kitchen conversation and pats the cushion of a small chair she has moved next to her, near the loveseat. I ask, "*Que piensa usted sobre mi hijo?*" What do you think of my son? "He's incredible," she responds in Spanish. "He's so curious and such an intelligent boy." Irma rejoins us, eager to officially start the interview process.

Two years earlier, I traveled to Cuernavaca, Mexico, to one of many Spanish language schools in an effort to prepare for this very moment. That experience and several years of basic Spanish in non-credited adult education classes resulted in my conversational, albeit choppy, command of the language.

"Have you cared for children before? Do you have any brothers and sisters? How will you discipline Miguel?" Throughout the questioning, Irma is anxious and hovers close by to ensure Paulina stays on point.

Having to rely solely on my Spanish, I'm nervous. I fire the questions so quickly at Paulina that she has little opportunity to respond. When I ask the third question about disciplining my three-year old son, she picks up Barbie's dog leash and smiles. I see Irma shoot a look of concern at her, but I quickly laugh, which calms us all.

Paulina and I share a similar sense of humor. It's been six weeks since Miguel has come to live with me, and there have been many challenges in our short time together. More than anything, I need someone who can laugh with me through the difficult times. Over the next several years my son will be a handful and test my will. I know I need to insulate his world with people who can love him and make him smile. I must provide him, for the first time in his life, a permanent commitment and the security that comes with that. He needs to move beyond anger and rage and be nurtured and loved. I need a nanny who can assist me on this journey, and one who laughs freely and has a great sense of humor will go a long way.

I learn so much this day. Paulina is twenty-nine years-old, and falls somewhere in the middle of her large family; she's one of many siblings. "They're like my own children." She smiles as she talks about growing up and caring for her youngest brothers and sisters.

She dreams of continuing her education and becoming an artist, but in reality had few options in Mexico. "I gave up my dreams," she says matter-of-factly. Instead, she worked as a secretary in Monterey, her hometown, several hours south of the Texas border. As a secretary, she made next to nothing; her husband, Sergio, was a waiter and made a bit more. Their life in Mexico was a constant struggle to survive, and as a result they had little to lose and everything to gain by moving to the United States.

Paulina repeats again and again that her true love is art; her true passion, painting. "I'm a creative person," she says proudly. "I am fully alive when I paint." All this talk of art and passion makes Irma nervous. Her practical side doesn't approve of such frivolous pursuits, and so she repeatedly redirects the conversation back to Paulina's maternal instincts. She reaffirms how caring and patient Paulina is with cousins who visit frequently. I, on the other hand, am excited about her creative talents and want to hear more. Like my son, she appears to love to use her hands. Both find satisfaction in creating an end product. Miguel can spend hours fixing, building, and creating a masterpiece. Although I am an active participant alongside my son, I often struggle to meaningfully contribute. Now perhaps he can have a partner who shares his interests and talents. The more I learn about Paulina, the more hopeful I grow about the prospects of our collaboration on Miguel.

I explain to both women I'm looking for someone to come to my home three days a week to help me with Miguel; there will be light cleaning and cooking involved. Ideally, the schedule would include two nights during the week and one full day on the weekend or about fifteen to twenty hours a week. I'll use a small stipend the state provides per month to care for Miguel and will earmark it to pay for our nanny. Without this extra money I couldn't swing this arrangement.

With the respite, I hope to have time to climb Squaw Peak or Camelback Mountain. Climbing urban mountains is what I do to hash out life's problems and parenting challenges, leaving them behind in a trail of dust and sweat. A little extra time will also allow me to run errands and grocery shop. Whatever help I receive at this point is welcomed. More important than the household chores, I explain, is that someone seamlessly picks up where I leave off on any given day, and keep my son meaningfully engaged. I realize this is no small order. Descriptions of "love" and "nurture" recall the role of mother; the importance of a female influence on my son's life dawns on me.

"It would be fun." Paulina summarizes the opportunity to work with Miguel. Fun sounds good. Each day I struggle to make sense of my new role as father. It's been intense and I've only just begun. My son is obstinate and challenges my authority, but mostly he's angry and defiant. As a result, I don't allow myself to live in the moment and laugh; I'm stressed out and worrying about all that may go wrong. I look over at my son as he plays with Barbie and Pepe and see he is happy. He's beyond happy; he's euphoric. This child has so much potential. I know I must be patient and surround myself with others who find the good in him. Paulina has a kind and gentle soul, and is quickly winning me over.

Logistically, Paulina reassures me that she's already mastered the bus lines in her short time in Phoenix, and points to a worn, dog-eared schedule on the nearby coffee table. On the drive over to meet Paulina, Miguel had asked about the small crowd of people huddled under the shade of an electronic sign in front of a corner bank building. "What are they doing? Are they lost?" Just above their heads, along with the time of day, the digital sign kept flashing 114 degrees, as if the scorching heat had broken the control mechanism. Scrunched in limited shade, wearily, the group waited for the next bus.

Although we live twenty miles apart, the trip is a straight shot. The bus will take her within walking distance of my house. I have never ridden a City of Phoenix bus. For me, it remains a last resort. From my comfortable vantage point, taking it in the extreme summer heat is inhumane. From Paulina's perspective, the bus is a blessing and her ticket to freedom. "I always meet interesting people," she says as if describing a daily adventure.

Paulina is very convincing. "The schedule is good," she reiterates. She has overcome all of my potential objections. On late nights, when the bus stops running, her husband will pick her up. I learn that Sergio works as a busboy, alongside his uncle, at a Mexican restaurant not far from our house. *Does she really know what she is getting into?* I wonder. Paulina remains unwavering as I describe Miguel's traumatic beginnings. The nomadic mother, the drugs, the abandonment, violence, exposure to possible abuse, and his volatile behavior in the foster home generate no visible signs of distress or unusual reaction. "I would be angry too," she says after my long diatribe. "He needs love. And a little fun won't hurt," she adds with a big smile. My heart is won over.

"Try her—you'll like her!" Aunt Irma chimes in a final endorsement, a large smile covering her face. Everything about this first meeting feels right. Paulina's connection with Miguel is real. I can see this as the two build some unknown structure from toothpicks. They sit at a small table just off from the kitchen. Their bodies touch as Paulina's weight spills over her chair, almost engulfing Miguel, who sits in the adjacent seat. He's comfortable with her and appears to enjoy the contact of her boundless skin. They look like mother and son. Now *I'm* smiling. As I watch the two of them, I realize that there are few things more powerful than someone else loving your own child. Indeed, Paulina will be a good choice.

I don't ask for references. Nor do I explicitly inquire if Paulina is living legally in this country, or if she has a valid work permit. Naively, I reason everything will work out.

SIX

The Magic Closet

I'm reminded of my first day of training to be a waiter, now so many years ago. At each table, I stand in her shadow, desperate to pick up tips and tools of the trade. How does she greet the customers? What are the abbreviations for the menu items? How do you make coffee?

The first couple of hours with Paulina are eye-opening and filled with valuable lessons. First and foremost, I seem to have missed the magic of the hall closet. To date, I have treated it as a resting spot for junk and other unimportant household items. However, within minutes of her arrival, Paulina and Miguel have hit the motherload. This little closet is where all the precious treasures lie. Pipe cleaners, poster board, glitter, flour, paint, and masking tape all come tumbling down. The two strike it rich with each shelf they uncover. I've forgotten half of this stuff was there.

All the while, Twister, Chutes and Ladders, Trouble, and a dozen other games sit idly by. "We can make it," I hear Paulina say effortlessly to Miguel's many requests. "It's easy." Paulina fully engages my son's imagination. I quickly learn she's all about making her own fun, and thus a perfect match for Miguel, who loves to invent and build. Better yet, Paulina loves to create from scratch.

In addition to the supplies from the magic closet, Paulina has quickly unearthed Halloween wigs, clothes, paint brushes, and perhaps the most unusual item, the chewing gum out of Miguel's mouth. Over the weekend, Miguel visited the circus and Paulina is now intent on making a *payaso* (clown) along with her new pupil.

As I sit and watch them work diligently, I realize how much I have to learn. Who would have thought chewing gum could be used to make a clown's nose? Paulina is a natural; everything is an adventure. And I struggle to identify who the real student is: father or son.

No more than two hours have passed when I stand face-to-face with two human-sized clowns named Jorge and Gumersinda. "*Que piensas?*" Paulina seeks feedback, while giggling with her small accomplice at her side. I recognize my clothes on Jorge and our mop on Gumersinda, but little else. How did she pull this off? My first real lesson in parenting is imparted today: less is more. How many toys are stacked in this little boy's closet? Miguel has spent several hours inventing and then constructing these clowns and not once has he missed those playthings built and packaged by someone else.

Watching Paulina play with Miguel, I reflect back on my first months as a parent. My approach couldn't have been more different or flawed. Those initial days were defined by a constant desire to move, rush everywhere and anywhere, Miguel almost always in tow. "We've got to get to Target today before it closes. Miguel, why did I need to go to the mall again? Let's go to the movies. Which one do you want to see?"

One Sunday, after volunteering in Miguel's preschool class at church, I stop at the gym. The place has a childcare center that allows parents to drop off their kids while they work out. *I really should do something special for Miguel today*, I keep thinking throughout my workout. By the time I'm done, it's already past 2:00 p.m. and he's logged a full day of activities. In the gym parking lot, as I am buckling him into his car seat, I ask, "Where do you want to go now? The park? A movie? McDonalds?" Miguel says simply, "I just want to go home and play with you."

Paulina isn't tormented by this same desire to rush. For her, multi-tasking is a foreign concept, and so there are no distractions competing with my son's playtime. She bestows her full attention upon Miguel and plays with such ease and simplicity. I marvel at her contentedness and yearn for the same sense of wholeness and focus.

Although I play with my son, it's not the same. The clock is never out of sight. It's always a negative attraction. I "give" Miguel fifteen minutes of play time and then I declare it's time to race to the grocery store. I "allow" myself twenty minutes to work with him on the computer, then I must go out and mow the lawn. Whenever we're together, I have one eye on the clock. I struggle to incorporate my son into our new life together, trying to fit my new parenting responsibilities around my old life, my old routine, rather than weave a new tapestry around our new and unchartered future. Like many parents, I convince myself that things are not going to dramatically change, but of course they do. Indeed, one time driving away from the gym I had the feeling I had forgotten something. This was confirmed when I looked back and saw an empty car seat. Frantically, I returned to the childcare center to reclaim my newly adopted son. Paulina, on the other hand, never takes her eye off the ball. There is something spiritual in her demeanor; you see it in her touch, you hear it in her tone. In her worldview, every day is new and changing. How can it not be with a three year old? This is not an act but rather an unspoken vocation; she truly wants to be nowhere else. She has purpose, an appreciation for living fully in the moment.

In Paulina's presence, it becomes clear that I have been scheduling Miguel like he's a client and booking him into appointments in my day planner accordingly. There's no reward for cutting our time short, no quarterly bonus for accomplishments while we share time together. There is no stock award at the end of the year for surpassing my goal. He's not my colleague or client—he's my son and he deserves my full attention.

As the Director of Public Relations for a growing home builder, I'm encouraged to juggle many tasks at once, to do more to drive sales. However, one thing is certain – there are no specific adoption benefits that allow for additional leave or compensation. Few companies are yet on the bandwagon recognizing adoption as a legitimate reason for further time off. As a result, my time away from work and with Miguel will be brief. Soon the eight weeks I have taken off through the Family Medical Leave Act will be over. Prior to Miguel's arrival, I maxed out my vacation and sick days to facilitate meetings with a variety of social workers and visitations at his foster home; those were necessary for certification. Money is tight and this adds to my stress level. For the first time, I am fully appreciating what it feels like to have another human be totally reliant on me.

As a result, the pressure builds with each passing day to lay more groundwork and to solidify the tenuous bond between us. My frenetic pace is an unconscious attempt to maximize the limited time the two of us have before I must go back to work. Although my salary affords me a middle class existence, adoption expenses have whittled away my small savings. There will be many future sacrifices to pay my bills. I will continue driving my aging Ford Explorer and tighten my belt in all areas. Requesting unpaid leave to lengthen the transition time is not an option. Miguel has a list of special needs that must be addressed, however, the resources needed to tackle them remains a mystery.

When I return to work it will be to a near impossible schedule. Miguel will be going to a Montessori daycare close to my office, yet far from our home. Several children of colleagues attend the school and all the parents highly recommend the hands-on curriculum. We'll wake by 5:30 a.m. and due to traffic, won't return most nights until 6:30 p.m. In calm moments, I convince myself things will work out. It always does. I'm fortunate my parents, two brothers, and extended family all live in Phoenix and can help pitch in. Watching Paulina seamlessly fit into our little family and the emerging routine brings me peace of mind and lifts a large weight from my shoulders. Of course, I can't help but worry about how Paulina will react at the first sign of a Miguel meltdown, but today there is no sign of a tirade.

At the end of the first night, I quietly return from the grocery store. It's bedtime and Paulina needs no cue from me to start the process. Miguel hates this time. The demons of his childhood linger and loom in the darkness of night. He fights the nightly routine and lies restlessly in bed. He pulls the sheets off in fits of rage, and gets up time and again to ensure that I have not abandoned him like so many have before in his short life.

Paulina doesn't hear me return. Feeling a bit like a Peeping Tom, I stand down the hall quietly and watch the two of them. Miguel has his pajamas on and is brushing his teeth. He laughs freely, the night demons nowhere to be found. "Do you like to sing?" Paulina asks in Spanish. The two sing a song about a crazy monkey who lives in the jungle. She does the first verse and Miguel repeats it back. They swing their arms like monkeys as they travel down the hall to Miguel's bedroom.

Instinctively, she picks him up; his head rests on her shoulder. Although small for his age, Miguel still weighs at least thirty-five pounds. She begins effortlessly rocking him slowly, while sweetly singing a song that repeats *mi amor* over and over. Miguel calms immediately. She continues for another fifteen minutes and my son tranquilly surrenders and falls asleep. I'm convinced that I'm in the presence of a full-blown child whisperer. In the past, I've spent hours putting this little boy to sleep. As she gently places him in bed, I struggle again to identify the student: my son or myself.

Paulina steps out of the room, and quietly closes the door. She lets out a small scream as she walks into the hallway. Seeing me smiling, she laughs. "*Miguel esta durmiendo,*" she says innocently. He is indeed sleeping and in less than one day he has grown attached to his new nanny. Paulina is in the process of resetting our gauges, calming the engines, and steering our ship in a new, more promising direction.

As we wait for Sergio to pick her up, she follows me to the living room where we begin to talk about her life. Her last job, she discloses, was a brief stint caring for several children of a family of Mexican nationals in Laredo, Texas. This was not a good situation.

The mother of the children looked down on Paulina and treated her poorly, "like a slave," she says. The mother imposed a caste system, making it clear to Paulina that she was somehow less worthy due to her residency status. As a result, the children failed to respect her. "I had to leave," Paulina says somberly. "It was unbearable."

Paulina talks about how eager she is to learn English and become more proficient on the computer. "I have a long list of classes I want to take," she says sounding like an excited school girl. She shares how much she loves attending the vocational school close to her aunt's house. She sees education as a privilege and wants to take advantage of all that she can. She enjoys meeting other students from Mexico, all of whom have migrated to Phoenix for a better life. Sergio encourages her and attends classes as well.

She confesses to hating secretarial work, although she told her family otherwise. Working as a secretary for next to nothing was a mental challenge. "It was so boring that a monkey could do my job," she laughs. At an early age, her family grew weary of her dreams to be an artist. Sergio, her husband, briefly studied medicine back home, but higher education in Mexico was never a reality for either of them. Plain and simple, Paulina states their prospects in Mexico were bleak. For both, living in the United States is all about opportunity. Paulina explains that she and Sergio have next to nothing in their new life, but hope. They will not trade this opportunity for anything.

At 10:00 p.m. there is a light knock on the front door. Sergio has arrived; I can see through the front window his small, beaten-up pickup truck. Grey primer covers several patches of metal. "*Mucho gusto*," Sergio says extending his hand. He is a likeable and friendly guy. "*El gusto es mio*," I shake his hand and respond in textbook Spanish. He's not much taller than Paulina, thin, and sports a mustache. The two laugh easily together. He joins us on the couch where we chat. Sergio shares with me that earlier in the day Paulina had repaired their DVD player. "*Ella es una mecanica*," he laughs. He tells me she is a mechanic at heart and definitely is the handier of the two. She loves to fix things and he encourages me to save up my home improvement projects for future visits. "She can fix anything," he says. Paulina elbows her husband to stop his boasting. She's red with embarrassment.

They are both adventurous. With so little to their name, it's easy for them to jump in their truck and explore new territory. Soon they'll visit Sedona and the Grand Canyon. They demonstrate a sense of optimism and freedom, and I feel fortunate our paths have crossed.

After Paulina and Sergio leave, I crawl into bed feeling energized about our time together. Within seconds, I hurl the covers away from me; I'm convinced something fuzzy is on my leg. In fact, I feel a lot of fuzzy somethings. This is significant. Phoenix residents far and wide are plagued by scorpions. These nocturnal spiders are notorious for hiding in bedding, closets, shoes, and other dark, cool places.

A wooden backscratcher now in hand for a weapon, I turn the lamp on at the nightstand. Quickly, I realize it's not scorpions that are hibernating, but rather, a final art project. While I was at the grocery store, Miguel and Paulina took all the remaining Q-tips in the house, made spiders, and then placed them in my bed, all designed to make me scream like a child. Their plan is an overwhelming success. Sometime later in the night, Miguel wakes me up, a huge smile on his face and asks: "Were you scared, Dad? Were you scared?"

SEVEN

Two Steps Forward, One Step Back

It's only a matter of time before Paulina experiences one of Miguel's meltdowns. I dread the reality but am certain he will eventually direct his anger at her. So far though, he saves it all for his father.

Authority appears to trigger instinctive rage. The more comfortable Miguel becomes with me and our new life together, the more difficult he gets. Although everyone around me says this makes sense, I still expect the opposite. As he transforms into a scrappy cage fighter, fading are the angelic behavior and sweet disposition. Each day he is set off by the smallest imposition or redirection. Though I dance around his ring of darkness and anger, there is almost no hope of escaping it. My son's transition is rocky at best, and harrowing at its worst.

When I take Miguel fishing at one of several city lakes, I'm surprised to learn that he likes it. His fleeting attention is replaced with a complete obsession to catch fish. After several hours and a number of close calls with bites falling off his hook, it's time for us to leave. It's hot and we're well overdue for lunch and a nap, yet Miguel refuses to budge. I give him several warnings that we'll soon be leaving, but in what is becoming a pattern, he looks at me with his eyes partially closed and tilts his head as if bating me to enforce the rules. His face is scrunched and distorted and looks like something out of *The Exorcist*. "NO!" he screams repeatedly in a creepy tone as I approach. "I hate you!" he shouts when I don't relent. Parents are looking at us as I work to bring this latest flare-up to an end. "That's it Miguel, we need to go," I say one final time as I reach out to grab him. He takes off running. Just before he reaches the busy four lane intersection, I tackle him. I have a hundred and fifty pounds on him, but it takes all my energy to hold him down and keep him from running into traffic.

Miguel has a seeming need to run and escape accountability; he wants to dodge any resulting consequences. Though so early in his young life, this behavior will define much of his future. He attempts to bite and scratch me, hoping to be set free. At this moment, he wants nothing more than to resurrect his goal of catching a fish, even if it means dying at the hands of a passing motorist.

He refuses to go into his child seat, which leaves me no other option than to pin him down and force the straps over his head. He flails to avoid succumbing to the loud clicking of the seatbelt, and looks at the lake as if he'll be back with fishing pole in hand any minute, just as soon as he's made his escape. I'm keenly aware of a group of concerned mothers who look at me as if I am a methodical child abuser. Miguel repeatedly spits at me and yells "I hate you" as I work his arms through the restraints. Spitting is a new tactic and just one of several that keep him fully committed to resistance.

Miguel doesn't fall asleep on the way home. In fact, far from it. He grabs hold of his treasured Spiderman fishing pole and begins breaking it into pieces. I pull into a parking lot across from the Super Kmart and open the back passenger door, screaming, "What are you doing?" As I reach for the pole, Miguel jabs me in the neck with the tip. I start bleeding from a long deep scratch, and grab the remains of the pole, forcing the small end out of his clenched fist. He's furious and kicks his arms and feet in hopes of landing a final blow.

I remove my t-shirt, mopping the blood from my neck as I head home. I muster up calm in my otherwise petrified voice and tell my three year-old that he will be in timeout when we return.

He screams nonstop throughout the remaining trip. Once home, I quickly wrestle him out of his car seat and head directly to his bedroom. I place him in the corner and remind him that he must remain seated for five minutes before he can come out. He's instantly up and throwing books at me once the door shuts. With no other tricks up my sleeve, I position myself to stand guard in the hallway; I breathe deeply but as quietly as possible, so he won't know that I'm just outside his door. I'm drenched in sweat from fear and the summer heat. For the next fifteen minutes, Miguel throws most of his belongings against walls and windows. Eventually the noise dies out as he falls asleep. I, too, lie down in the cool dark hallway and rest.

To the many who ask "How's it going?" I respond confidently, a smile plastered on my mannequin-like face. "It's amazing!" They believe me and why shouldn't they? I say it with such positive conviction that at times even I believe it. "It's the best thing I've ever done – a dream come true."

The truth is that I'm terrified, scared shitless, and most times feel downright disoriented and afraid to admit it to anyone. After only a few months, there remains a nagging, reoccurring reservation that I've made the biggest mistake of my life; of course, I feel guilty for even having such thoughts. *It will get better*, I chant mindlessly throughout my day. It can't possibly get any worse. Can it? *I can do this*, I constantly reassure myself. I need to bite the bullet and make it through. I count each day as a rite of passage. Since Miguel's arrival, I mark each passing week off the calendar. I made it. We made it. Most days, this is the only tangible sign of progress.

Every day, I rummage through the adoption file that Cyndi gave me months earlier, searching for some meaning and context. Although there is much to explain Miguel's uneven behavior, there's no roadmap for moving forward. How is a parent to deal with unbridled rage? I find several reports in which social workers hypothesize that Miguel has never learned to trust because he's never been the beneficiary of unconditional love. As a result, he fights authority and resists affection and love, all in an effort to win. In a strange way, he's a gifted fighter. I was unrealistic when I gave myself only two months to tame and calm this small tormented soul before returning to work. Now, past this deadline, I refuse to entertain the notion that it may very well take a lifetime. Miguel's daily chorus of "I hate you" shields him from loving me or anyone who must serve as an authority figure. To survive as a family, we must learn to respect and love one another.

Equally important, Miguel must learn to socialize with other children. He doesn't have to master this feat, but he can't continue to bite and hit like he does now whenever he doesn't get his way. He must be able to attend school but his uncontrollable outbursts put this in jeopardy. After his second week, the director of the Montessori school reports major problems. Miguel is biting the students and the teachers. On several occasions, I've had to leave work early to meet with teachers and staff. Fortunately, the director is also the parent of several children who were part of the state system and she understands. "You will get through this but it will take some time," she counsels. "Our first priority is to figure out how to stop the biting so the other children are not in harm's way." She is put in an impossible situation genuinely wanting to help Miguel but also needing to protect her other students, teachers, and parents.

Miguel fights most things, but timeout and naps are at the top of the list. At the slightest hint of either, he launches into battle with a fury that is unnerving. He kicks and bites when I attempt to redirect his anger. Everything is an overreaction and when furious, he gravitates toward destruction. I can only guess he feels a freedom from breaking things, as though he's attempting to right the wrongs of his life. Through this acting out, he seems to feel empowered. I do my best to remain strong and look unbreakable. However, more often than not I am left wondering: is he winning?

At some point through his belabored bedlam, when he decides he is completely purged of these tortuous outbursts, Miguel becomes calm and sweet. When it finally comes, the transition is instant. Seemingly, he is free from his inner turmoil. The only reminders are the debris and chaos around him, and his father's battle scars. Through these tantrums, he expels the demons; the evil that was predicated by the many who abandoned him, but not before neglecting and abusing him.

His destructive cycle repeats itself throughout our days together. It's like watching the same scary movie, a hellish remake of *Ground Hog's Day*. This is our "normal"—we know no other. Whether the morning fishing trip, play-dates, family gatherings, picnics, or weekend getaways, they're all ripe for a major meltdown. I'm too new at this to comprehend if I'm doing something wrong or if this has some official diagnosis other than "rocky transition." I blame myself for not being able to fend off Miguel's anger, and as a result refuse to share the full anguish with family and friends. At times, I feel like a massive failure. This can't be what every new parent experiences. Can it? It feels like the terrible twos, only, so much worse.

I worry that Cyndi might label me "unfit" and so I don't fully disclose all the details or my inner turmoil. For better or worse, I won't allow them to brand me as weak or incapable. Technically, I am still on probation; legally, I'm viewed as just another foster parent. I must find a way to mend this brokenness, to build my resilience, and to protect my feelings. I must battle better by creating an armor to protect my feelings. Currently, Miguel has the upper hand. His poker chips pile up with each passing day. What makes this all the more difficult are the many who envision an impossible fairy tale. My own story cries out for a clean and happy ending: single father searches for needy son and the two live happily ever after. Most of the time, I'm unconvinced the two of us will make it through another day, never mind a lifetime.

• • •

We're stepping out of the pool as Paulina arrives. She begins making tacos, Miguel's favorite meal. She is a welcome sight. Quietly, I recap the day's conflict, as Miguel changes from his bathing suit. She looks concerned as she checks the wound on my neck. She's now fully invested as my comrade, my fellow foot soldier. We're both in the trenches; both trying to navigate this little soul to safety. As a result, I feel stronger when she is present. We have become friends and feel closeness like family.

Standing on a chair in the kitchen, Miguel is Paulina's helper. He squeezes the ground beef through his fingers and browns the meat, just as Paulina has taught him. She's right in step with the Montessori method, which stresses hands-on learning. Rather than watch him cutting tomatoes with the sharp knife, I leave the room. Miguel feels like he's in charge, as if he's the boss. This is his kitchen and this, his meal. He's in control and as a result, content.

After dinner, Paulina becomes his target. Miguel is angry and upset at her. He wants her to show him how she makes her high-flying paper airplane, but she's busy cleaning up from dinner and pulling together laundry. She says she'll sit with him when she's done. From the backyard, I see him throw something at her. Ignoring the outburst, she walks away, refusing to engage. He follows her around the house as she goes about her business. "Paulina, how do you make the wings?" he asks holding the paper. She remains silent, still unwilling to provoke the featherweight boxer. "Paulina, how do you get the plane to fly so high?" still, no response. Five or six more questions are fired off and met with silence. Miguel finally relents and heads back to the kitchen table to begin folding planes without her. Awaiting Paulina's return, he works quietly and productively.

Near sundown, I pull Miguel in his red wagon several short blocks to the desert preserve. This is our nightly ritual. We visit the many rabbits and birds that fill the desert. If nothing else, we have a routine. Each night, the "bird lady" brings a large bucket of seeds and fruit, cut into small pieces. She has taken a liking to Miguel and lets him throw the fruit to the rabbits. These nightly escapes serve as a peaceful timeout and also reinforce the importance of repetition that Miguel has never experienced. This place is our sanctuary.

Tonight, Paulina joins us. She wears white tennis shoes from a local drug store and a baggy men's red t-shirt. Excitedly, she talks of her recent trip to Sedona. Soon she'll paint the red rock formations on canvas. Miguel runs ahead, attempting to catch cottontail rabbits as they dart across the trail. She tells me of her plan to bring Miguel to the nursery later in the week. The two will plant new flowers in the front courtyard. We laugh at the thought of Miguel getting dirty as only little boys can. We hear the sounds of doves as they rustle through Mesquite trees, and lizards darting through desert ground cover. As we turn a corner, we scare a large group of quail from the trees. Rabbits dart everywhere as Miguel runs toward them. He's determined to catch one before sunset. We throw handfuls of seeds to the growing crowd of hungry birds.

We begin the short walk home and encounter a beautiful sunset, brilliant with yellow, red, and orange, over a landscape of blue sky. The lingering heat leaves the desert serene. Miguel happily talks to himself and his group of imaginary cottontail rabbits that he's lined up on both sides of his wagon. Unburdened by his past, he is light and easy to pull. Paulina and I are quiet. I'm struck by the contrast. Our day was defined by full blown chaos; now a prolonged peace settles on this deserted street we call home. The scales ever-so-slowly tipping, the routine is gradually taking hold. The repetition and stability are breaking down illogical resistance. Love is slowly penetrating my wounded but wonderful little soldier.

It's bedtime and Miguel is tired. I turn the last page of *Curious George*, and he's tranquil, content, and near sleep. From nowhere, he begins describing in amazing detail his half-brother Javier and him sitting in the setting sun, the two alone on a curb along a busy city street. This is the first time he has talked of Javier since coming to live with me. At that time, Miguel was just 2 ½ years old, his brother, ten months younger. He talks of protecting Javier as various strangers approach. "They were bad people," he says haltingly. He talks of hearing gunfire and boys fighting on the street. Eventually, two women sat with them until the police arrived.

How many stories are locked away in this tortured soul? This boy has lived more than most adults do in a lifetime. It all begins to make sense: the frustration, the uncontrollable anger, and the hateful outbursts. On this night I recommit to do all I can to give Miguel every possible chance to succeed. He deserves nothing less.

Many believe wounds inflicted this young will never mend. Tonight, I refuse to buy into that line of thinking. I'm not alone. Paulina is proving to be an important part of the remedy. Regardless of Miguel's anger, she's there to apply unconditional love to my young son's wounds. Most importantly, I am learning.

"What a day!" I recap for my brother Kevin, who calls me minutes before I drift off to sleep. He's on a business trip in California and is checking up on me. He senses I am weary. I tell him about the fishing trip gone wrong, the broken pole, and the destruction that remains in his room. With two boys of his own, he laughs. He's exactly what I need at this moment. "At least Miguel is adopted," he chuckles. "You have an excuse for his behavior, but what's the excuse for my two?" It feels good to laugh again.

EIGHT

Day Tripper

Taking the entire week off is not an option; I have to work. I have no more vacation or sick time to cover the five days Miguel will be off for Fall Break. With my savings account fully depleted, I'm already counting on next year's tax return to make up for growing credit card debt. We've recently visited a well-respected child psychologist at Phoenix Children's Hospital to gain additional insights into Miguel's learning and emotional disabilities, which greatly impacts upon his academic progress and further agitates his overall well-being. These appointments with specialists are expensive and not covered by insurance. Each meeting invariably leads to more testing and more specialists and more money, which creates more stress.

Although my boss is supportive, his wife has always been a homemaker. Even now that their children are in college, this traditional perspective at times clouds his understanding of my current dilemma. I've been careful not to go to the well too often by arriving late or missing important meetings unless it's absolutely necessary. More often than not I'll take a longer lunch or leave with a pile of work under my arm to complete at night at home in an effort to make time to visit Miguel at school or take him to his many appointments. Because Miguel's preschool doesn't offer childcare during school holidays, I'm left to pull a rabbit from my hat to ensure he's covered. This situation has played out when he's sick or had an ill-timed meltdown.

The day before Fall Break, a group of mostly stay-at-home moms gathers in a tight circle. One mother is proudly passing around a spreadsheet that reads, "Ashley's Fall Break." Peering over the shoulders of one of the women, I sneak a quick glimpse of Monday's activities. "The Zoo" and "Trip to Library" are the featured events. Highlighted in yellow for Wednesday afternoon is "Tea With Mommy – Ritz Carlton." Shamelessly, I eavesdrop on their discussion as they busily plan activities for the break. In fact, several of the moms suggest meeting up with Ashley and her mother at the Ritz Carlton for a tea party. "The more the merrier," Ashley's mom sings out. She's giddy with excitement about the prospect of the impromptu gathering. Not interested in reading the schedule farther, I conclude I'm definitely behind the eight ball; I have planned little beyond a trip to our neighborhood McDonald's Playland.

These moments remain a wake-up call, but fortunately I'm a quick study. I'm learning that the "Mommy Network" is a valuable resource for unlocking all sorts of important information, from identifying the best teachers to picking sports teams with great coaches. I exploit my status as a single dad to generate sympathy and gain essential information. So far, the strategy has paid off. These women have been generous with their knowledge. Most recently, I found Miguel's pediatrician, a godsend, through this informal network.

But I feel caught between two worlds. These mothers are in complete control of their children's social and activity calendars. Play-dates, carpools, and sports practices are scheduled solely through them. For the most part, dads are hands-off at the school, unless it involves the occasional parent-teacher conference or open house. The dads seem more than happy to delegate the daily logistics of raising their children to their wives, while they coach Little League baseball and Pop Warner football. At times, I'm envious of this clear division of labor, because I wear both hats. As a result, these moms and dads are uncertain to which side I owe my allegiance, and I struggle with this as well. Couples invite other couples and their children to barbeques and swim parties. Miguel and I are excluded and sometimes I feel like the odd man out.

I'm saved by Paulina, who is happy to care for Miguel for the entire break. This is significant, because my parents, who recently retired, left weeks earlier on a trip of a lifetime with their new travel trailer and pick-up truck, their shiny new kayaks securely fastened above the cab. They plan to explore much of what lies between Arizona and New Jersey, where both were born and raised, and aren't scheduled to return for several months.

I'm excited for them. As a new parent, I'm finally beginning to appreciate all their sacrifices raising me and my brothers. My dad, who was most concerned about leaving his job and having too much time on his hands, is beginning to blossom in retirement. "I don't know how I ever found time to work," he says of his new schedule. His grandchildren fill much of his spare time, and with each new one, his tough exterior softens. As a grandparent he's affectionate and gentle, and his emotions are more expressive and visible than ever. Although his retirement holds uncertainty with a recent diagnosis of prostate cancer, he stops by often just to get a hug from his grandson or sneak him out to McDonald's for a hot fudge sundae. He loves watching him on the indoor playground, while he trades off reading the paper and chasing Miguel.

Paulina is less structured than the mothers from school. She prefers to let Miguel's interests guide their time together. With us now for more than five months, she's more than capable of keeping him engaged with a variety of spur-of-the-moment projects, all creative and captivating.

Paulina arrives at 6:30 a.m. on Monday, the start of Fall Break, and describes her plan for the day, which includes a ride on the city bus, an urban fieldtrip of sorts. Miguel has been asking for weeks for just such an outing. He's envious each time we drop Paulina off at the bus stop, and desperate to be seated next to his nanny. Waiting for her to board, we wave through clouds of exhaust. Be it school or city bus, Miguel is determined to ride one of these huge machines, so I agree to the agenda. And, why shouldn't I? Paulina travels this route frequently with no issues. In a matter-of-fact manner, she explains they'll take the bus to her house and return in time for dinner. The plan is simple and straightforward. Although I have lingering concerns about the bus ride and some of the neighborhoods they will be traveling through, I brush them aside as I rush out the door. Throughout the day I give the two little thought. I'm busy at work and lost in various projects. On my way home I call ahead; there's no answer.

As I enter, the house is dark and quiet. This is unusual and a clue that something is wrong. There will be no panic until I investigate further, but my mind races, which triggers my heart to accelerate. "Miguel? Paulina?" I call out, sounding mildly confident. "Where can they be? It's after 7:00," I reason aloud. "They're always home by now!"

With each passing room, there's no sign of my son. I struggle to recall any important details of our parting conversation. I run to Miguel's bedroom and push the door open. "Miguel? Miguel, where are you?" I yell out as panic jumps from my skin. I race to the backyard, which is dark. I sprint to the pool. Although it's gated and locks automatically, I'm undeterred. I unlock the gate and methodically walk the perimeter, sweeping the bottom for any signs of life. Unsatisfied with the first pass, I run back to the pump area and turn on the pool light. Illuminated a brilliant blue, the pool is vacant.

My god, what have I done? I backtrack in thought. "Focus on the details...focus, focus, focus," I repeat aloud. Leaning against the pool gate, I begin dismantling Paulina's credibility. What do I really know about her? Anyone seeing these two sitting together on a city bus would assume a routine outing between a mother and son. No one would suspect a potential kidnapping. In reality, it is I who has been questioned suspiciously about the Hispanic child at my side. Recently, I was trailed by mall security and asked where I was taking the screaming Hispanic boy I had securely by the hand.

Through the spiraling panic, my thoughts are further deteriorating. Is Paulina the ringleader of some baby broker cartel? I lock the pool gate and head for the metal shed, which houses the lawnmower and has become the dumping ground for paint cans and toxic chemicals from previous owners. *Oh god, don't let him be here.* Seemingly ever off their tracks, I slide the squeaky, wobbly metal doors open. It's dark and I grab for the rake and stab blindly at the floor of the shed to ensure there are no unknown objects on the ground. Mercifully, all is clear inside the shed. In my mind, a detailed hijacking plot marinates. I imagine that Miguel, who can easily fit within a burlap sack, is now being forced under the baseboards of Sergio's truck, and likely passing across the Arizona border, soon to be lost deep in the far reaches of Mexico. Although far-fetched, stranger things have happened.

A coworker has recently relayed a harrowing story of a Mexican national, who has been staying in her guesthouse. In lieu of rent, he works and does chores around her home. The handyman has become much more than a boarder and over time is now like a member of their family, so much so that she jokingly calls him her "house hubby." Even her husband has grown to love him and treats him like one of their grown children. Things went horribly wrong for their friend on a return trip back from Mexico. As he attempted to cross the U.S. border after visiting his wife and children, the man was denied re-entry—he'd apparently violated a condition of his Mexican travel visa. His only option was to pay a coyote, a human smuggler, to transport him across the border and deliver him back to Phoenix. During the summer months in Arizona, coyotes are responsible for countless deaths. They're notorious for leaving their human cargo in the desert to fend for themselves at the first sign of danger. Regularly, local news stations report the deaths of immigrants found throughout the desert of Southern Arizona. In fact, most years more than 200 Mexican nationals die this way in Arizona, many in search of their American dream.

A coyote forced my friend's handyman under floorboards of a truck in an effort to cross the border undetected. Once in

Phoenix, he changed the conditions of release, holding him at gun-point along with several others, including women and children, in a drop house in West Phoenix. The couple was contacted by the coyote and agreed to pay a $1,200 ransom for their friend's release. Carrying a Glock for protection, the husband met the kidnappers in a Westside Phoenix neighborhood, in front of a familiar grocery store chain, all as shoppers unknowingly paraded by the car during the tense exchange. Unwavering, my coworker's husband clarified to the coyote on his cell phone no money would change hands unless their friend was first released unharmed. Dazed and dehy-drated, he surfaced from a van across the parking lot.

Although that horrible story ended well, at this moment I have no idea where my son is and when he will return. Mexico is a huge country and he could be anywhere. I only know that Sergio and Paulina claim to be from Monterrey. "I never asked for references!" I scream out. "There is no one to blame, but myself." *How did I hire a complete stranger and never check her references?* I have spent more time hiring people at work than my own child's caregiver. Not to mention that I never followed up with any members of Paulina's extended family, or with the family in Laredo, Texas that she claimed to have briefly been employed by. Maybe the fam-ily discovered something sinister about her and consequently fired her in the process. In reality, I've only known Paulina for several months. I've worked diligently for years to adopt my son and now, carelessly, I allowed a complete stranger to snatch him away.

In the metal shed, hands resting on my knees, I am sweating and breathing heavy. The night air is heavy, and though the shed is like a sauna, I refuse to leave. I'm punishing myself for bungling this. It's here that I first detect a faint high-pitched noise coming from inside the house. It's clearly recognizable. It's unmistakably Miguel's favorite whistle. I hear the familiar sound again.

I run for the house as the whistle grows louder. Heading to the master bedroom, I throw on the lights, but am disappointed to find nothing. Diving to the floor, I see that the space under bed is bare. Just then, several toots come from the master bathroom.

Racing that way, past the closet, wedged in the corner of the walk-in shower is Paulina, all 300-plus pounds, and my son hiding behind her large skirt. "*Hola!*" Paulina says with a lilt in her voice. She and Miguel are laughing hysterically. I'm soaking wet and gasping for air, but I laugh. Tears drain from my eyes in relief. "*Sorpresa?*" Paulina asks. That's an understatement. I am surprised, but also hugely disappointed in myself. How quickly I betrayed Paulina, doubting her character and commitment to my son. It's this very game of hide-and-seek that is the main reason I have grown to love her. Paulina marches to her own beat. She's not afraid to think like a child and play like one too. How can I be angry at someone who is filled with so much love for my son?

Miguel is bursting with energy when he tells me about his day. "Dad, we met a man who couldn't see!" Miguel shares eagerly as the three of us sit on my bed. "We helped him get on the bus." Overflowing with excitement, he describes their activities and sounds more like he's spent the day at an amusement park than riding city buses. Miguel is not a kid to plop in front of a television or computer; he has the spirit of an intrepid explorer. Reliving his journey reminds me that each day is a new beginning for all children, and my son is no exception. There's no dread of tomorrow, but rather an excitement about the next great expedition.

"There was this mommy who had lots of kids and no money. Paulina gave her money." Miguel smiles upward at his travel companion. Paulina comments about how impressed she is with Miguel. On the bus ride home, he helped quiet one of the children of a distressed mother who was trying to feed her baby while tending to her two other children.

Not every parent would encourage such an outing, I know, but it is clear that Paulina has more on her lesson plan than killing time over tea at the Ritz. From what I gather, the two had the time of their lives. They stopped at Paulina's house briefly, but only to feed her dog and check in on her aunt, who was sick with the flu. Afterward, they re-boarded the bus and went to the downtown terminal, where Paulina gave Miguel a few dollars to buy snacks and miniature toys. While there, they walked the downtown streets and marveled at the architecture and skyscrapers. They rode the glass elevator to the top floor at the Hyatt and listened to street musicians playing guitars and singing folk songs near the bus terminal.

Miguel shares more details. He and Paulina met some of the homeless people who tend to congregate around the bus terminal. They stopped and talked with mothers and their children. *Could one of those women have been Miguel's mother?* When I've walked those same streets, I have looked in the faces of homeless Hispanic women with small children and wondered.

From what I know about Miguel's initial start in life, his mother was nomadic and relied on buses and friends for transportation. Her life was defined by her addictions and street omens. When things were bad, times got desperate. She abandoned her children frequently with strangers, and then CPS returned them to her parents. Over time, siblings were placed with paternal family members, more often with foster families because a father could not be identified. Miguel and his half-brother, Javier, became wards of the court after their maternal grandparents threw in the towel. The grandparents described the boys' behavior as "out-of-control" and as a result they relinquished any future responsibility. We recently visited Javier, who has been placed with a couple who have a daughter they adopted from the state system several years ago. Javier's parents—his father an architect and his mother a mortgage broker—are planning a move to Flagstaff. We're committed to staying in touch and Javier and his family will attend Miguel's upcoming fourth birthday party.

The remainder of Fall Break is less eventful but no less inventive. When she arrives Wednesday morning, Paulina is met by Miguel, who is clutching a group of animal pictures he's gathered for her. He's convinced the two need to build a zoo and as a result they create a plan.

As I drive away, I see Paulina trailing Miguel, pulling his red wagon. They're in a hunt for exotic game, digging through the many desert rocks, big and small, seeking out those that most resemble

Miguel's animal pictures. These rocks are anything but barren to Paulina; they serve as another palette for her art.

At lunchtime I call home. The zoo project is well underway, and they've just returned from gathering up all the available prickly pear fruit from our neighbors. Miguel shares that the two are making jam. It's nearing teatime at the Ritz Carlton. I again imagine the girls and their mothers all dressed up for the special occasion. I can't help but feel Miguel's got the best seat in the house.

The bond between two kindred souls grows deeper this week. Never leaving the neighborhood, Miguel is having a ball with his nanny and playmate. On Friday night, we drive Paulina to her bus just before it departs. Afterward, we stop at the drug store. As I wait in line at the pharmacy, Miguel runs down the toy aisle. When I find him, he's looking over posters of rock bands, teen idols, and pin-up models in swimsuits. Miguel lands on Christie Brinkley in a two-piece bathing suit. She's sweaty and tan and is posing on a beach in some unknown tropical location. "Paulina is not like this lady," says Miguel. "She's bigger." I say nothing and wait. "I like Paulina better," Miguel concludes. He reaches for my hand and we leave the store.

NINE

Lost and Found in Translation

It's 1:43 a.m. on a Saturday morning in early December, and I am a mess. Already sick, I'm on a steep decline with every passing hour. I drag my comforter into the bathroom and lie against the vanity directly across from the toilet, afraid that if I stray too far I won't make it back. Throwing up is inevitable. It's not a matter of if; only when. I hover over the bowl miserably, anticipating a violent upheaval. I'm desperate for relief that is too slow in coming. I must be better by morning—anything less just won't do. Devoid of energy, not even strong enough to panic, I rest my head on my hands over the toilet seat and close my eyes.

When I wake an hour later, I calculate that I've got less than eight hours before a dozen or more of Miguel's playmates and their parents, along with family and friends, begin showing up at our doorstep. They're coming to celebrate Miguel's fourth birthday. I've hired Ms. Susana, Miguel's P.E. teacher, who has a side business offering backyard gymnastics parties; she's scheduled to arrive at 9:30 a.m. with her equipment. Ever the perfectionist, I have a long list of items that must be done, including cleaning the very toilet that I hang my head over. One way or the other, this show must go on. Whether it is because it's our first birthday together or I'm making up for lost time, this party is important to me.

After only six months, Paulina is an integral part of our family. She's meeting many of my friends for the first time. Preparations for the party have been underway over the last week—Miguel and Paulina have made an elaborate clown piñata out of balloons and paper mache for the kids to crack open with Miguel's whiffle ball bat. Manny, the piñata, hangs from our foyer light just inside the front door.

"You're not serving beer and pretzels to the kids are you?" my friend jokes with me over lunch. He and his wife will be attending with their son, who is Miguel's age. My friend's wife has a talent for making parties look easy—dinners, birthdays, and informal mixers are of Martha Stewart caliber. My friend is a fixture at the grill, while his wife serves appetizers and facilitates mingling among guests. Her house is spotless and their son incredibly well mannered. I find myself competing with these idyllic images of husband and wife as though I must measure up, yet there's no wife in the picture dutifully planning and doting over the many domestic details. Despite the obstacles, and even as I struggle to remain coherent, I am resolved to pull off the party without a hitch.

"Honey, don't you want to cut back on a few activities?" My mom's voice echoes through my delirium, reverberating off the toilet bowl. Hours earlier she had called to check on the status of the party preparations. Undoubtedly, I have set a high standard for myself, well beyond what any mental health practitioners would deem healthy. Camping out over my toilet would be a perfect time to make last minute modifications, although I refuse to entertain such thoughts. I remain distracted and transfixed by my reflection in the water – a St. Bernard dog, drool pouring from my mouth. There will be no downgrading, no change from the original party agenda. In addition to gymnastics, Miguel and his friends will be making necklaces out of beads, a favorite activity of the birthday boy. Thereafter, the large group will launch into a series of traditional games, including a three-legged race, tug-of-war, an egg toss, sack race, bean bag toss, and finally, the piñata. Sometime along the way there will be a special guest appearance by a friend who has agreed to come dressed as Mickey Mouse. "Is it a problem if Mickey smokes?" he asked, when signing on for the task.

Desperate for this ill feeling to retreat, but too weak to fight it, I spread out on the bathroom floor and close my eyes. Fueled by anxiety, I dream frenetically. Kids are screaming everywhere as unruly four year-olds run wildly throughout the house. Manny, the clown piñata, has taken on human form and attacks the smallest children with a butcher knife. I am too sick to intercede. The little boy who sits next to Miguel at school now quietly hides under my bed. It all makes no sense. He's terrified that he'll be discovered by the crazed killer piñata. From my vantage point, only I can see Miguel's playmate under the bed. He hears the screams of his friends and covers his ears. As my face rests flatly against the cold bathroom floor, the small child looks at me, and silently pleads for help. I panic and search for answers. Why is this happening? Why aren't the surrounding parents doing anything to help? Why is Manny drinking a Diet Coke? Still unable to move, I scream out for the parents to acknowledge the chaos, but all remain in conversation, oblivious to the mayhem that surrounds them. I exchange a final terrifying glance with the boy, just before Manny pulls his small frame from under the bed. As the boy screams, I awake, struggling to breath. Disoriented, I bolt up and look at my alarm clock; it's now 3:05 a.m., which leaves me just over six hours.

The sickness begins in earnest. Again and again, I heave, drenched in sweat. With nothing left to expel, my abdominal muscles painfully constrict. My fever persists, my teeth chatter, and my body aches all over. I stumble back to my bed and pull the comforter over my head to create a tent-like effect to block out any light and the ever-present cold.

This time, I dream a vivid memory of my father, which has been a trend lately. I'm eleven and it's one of the many times I volunteer to ride shotgun and help him, a foot soldier in the war against hunger, bring food to the poor through an outreach program. On this trip, we help a farm-worker and his large family make it through to the end of the month, when his next paycheck arrives. Several times a year, our church, Our Lady of the Valley, held a canned food drive among parishioners for St Vincent De Paul, a charitable arm of the Catholic Church—the poor of the community were the beneficiaries. Back in the day, the homeless were not positioned on major intersections throughout Phoenix with cardboard signs pleading their cases in front of the court of public opinion. Children were not taught to shun the homeless or worse yet interrogate the downtrodden on the validity of their despair. The lesson then was simple: help those in need.

As if falling from a time machine, I wake with a start at 6:30 a.m. and need to process where I am. Chills and fever linger. Looking through my bedroom window onto the front lawn, I see a blanket of white resting gently upon the green winter rye grass. Snow is falling peacefully. *Am I hallucinating?* A Phoenix snow-storm is unheard of. In fact, I can't remember a single time the city has received visible snowfall within its limits. From time to time, the outlying desert foothills get a light dusting, but not the heavy dose that rests everywhere outside. The entire scene is surreal.

Canceling the party today is out of the question. I'll clean out my garage and set up the gymnastics equipment there. The solution will be time-consuming but doable. Rain or shine, there will be a birthday party. I have much to learn about little kids, but I do know that it wouldn't much matter to them whether they were in a dump or a garage, as long as they were free to run, scream, and jump on a trampoline.

Not usually one to languish in my own self-pity, I'm convinced that a warm shower will shake off my symptoms once and for all. I have much to do and too little time. I begin to shiver as I wait for hot water, my fever building yet higher. As a survival mechanism, I wrap a towel around me like a blanket. Minutes pass without warm water. Naked, I run to the garage, leaving tracks of wet footprints in my wake. I swing open the garage door to find steamy water flooding the concrete floor and pouring out from the bottom of the hot water heater. The river of water has left everything wet and damp in its wake. I manage to locate the valve and shut it off, which stops the flow of hot water. Discouraged, I sit naked on the stoop. My butt rests in warm water; it feels good. I rest my head on my knees. I'm covered in goose bumps, but remain grounded by the steam of the warm water rising against my bare skin.

When the doorbell rings, I make a beeline, unclothed, from the garage to my bedroom. I cup my private parts as I run past the front door with the long narrow glass panes. I throw on jeans and a heavy jacket, zipping it closed over my bare chest. "Coming, I'm coming!" I scream out. Opening the door, I am surprised to see Paulina. "*Puedo ayudarte?*" Invited to the party as a guest, Paulina now stands before me two hours early, eager to pitch in and help. Her early arrival will prove to be the best gift of the day. She looks at me with concern. "*Estas Enfermo?*" She asks if I am sick.

We head to the garage where she immediately picks up a broom and begins sweeping out the warm water. Miguel remains sound asleep as I call my father and plead. "Dad, can you help me out before the party begins?" Just blocks away, he'll be over in minutes. I walk barefoot in the snow as I move box after box to the side of the house and out of the sightline of guests. My pant legs are wet and covered in patchy snow. Ms. Susana is due any minute.

The doorbell rings again. It's beginning to feel more like a circus than a birthday party. From the moment he arrives, my dad seems out of sorts; something is definitely bothering him. With his mammoth blue toolbox in hand, he heads directly to the garage to assess the damage. With less than an hour before the party, the two of us argue whether the tank can be replaced in time. We compromise and agree to move the hot water tank out of the garage and replace it tomorrow. The last time we spoke, our conversation was strained, but he sounded upbeat about attending Miguel's birthday. I've noticed over the last couple weeks he's been stopping by less frequently, and when he does he seems uncomfortable.

"*Hola, Señor Waldron.*" Paulina greets my dad enthusiastically. "*Hola,*" he responds awkwardly. He's grown embarrassed to speak with Paulina. This is not the same man I remember negotiating fish and shrimp with the local Mexican fishermen. Through broken

Spanish he enjoyed engaging the locals in their native language. His mechanical abilities save him from any further discomfort as he focuses on the task at hand. Hearing his grandpa's voice, Miguel wakes up. He darts through the garage door in his dinosaur pajamas and hugs my dad. Paulina follows and soon swallows Miguel up in a huge hug.

"*Que pasó, Paulina? Que pasó?*" Miguel asks her what has happened as my dad and I wheel the broken hot water heater out of the garage. Miguel is desperate to know why there is water everywhere; his curiosity overwhelms him. Months before, Miguel would have peppered his grandpa with these questions, not Paulina. However, since her arrival, Miguel is speaking more Spanish than English when she's present. I note the look on my father's face as Miguel speaks rapidly to Paulina. He's unable to understand them as they carry on like mother and son.

I throw old beach towels and rags onto the garage floor as we go about drying the concrete surface. My dad disappears after mentioning something about fixing the leaky faucet in the guest bathroom. Just then, Ms. Susana drives up in a small pick-up truck. We pitch in to help her set up her equipment. Miguel jumps on the mini-trampoline; he's joyful and ecstatic, and loves the feeling of freedom from vaulting his small body through the air. Out of the corner of my eye, I notice my father getting into his truck. He's scheduled to return with my mom in less than an hour for the party, but has failed to say goodbye. I run toward the truck to thank him for once again saving the day. "Your kid is being raised by a complete stranger," he says as he rolls up the window and drives away. I watch his tires make fresh tracks as the snow continues to fall lightly on my bare feet.

"Give him time," my mom says as I quickly replay the scene. She is the interpreter and peacekeeper between my father and me. Our conversation is short because my dad will soon return home. "He's feeling like a stranger," my mom phrases delicately. "Honey, you need to be patient and try understanding his viewpoint."

She's right. No sooner did I adopt a son than I introduced a Spanish speaking nanny. I've done little since to help my father ease his discomfort. My mom reminds me that prior to Paulina, my dad enjoyed stopping over to visit his new grandson several times a week. It was easy and uncomplicated, and most importantly, he didn't have to think twice about how he would communicate to his grandson or his babysitter. Although grandparents are not supposed to have favorites, my dad and his newest grandchild share a unique bond. They're kindred spirits. At the first sight of his grandpa, Miguel is barely able to contain his excitement. They spend entire days in the garage working on electronics and woodworking projects. My dad has finally identified the perfect student to pass on his technical skills.

Now, competing for Miguel's attention with Paulina, my dad is struggling to identify his role. "Things are different and that's always hard for your father," my mom wisely reminds me. She reassures me it will all work out. "He'll come around, honey. Everyone loves Paulina!"

Undeniably, it was my dad who instilled compassion within me. I never doubt my mom's observation that his challenge has less to do with Paulina and more about his own changing role within our family dynamic. His legacy stands on his actions, more so than his words.

Miguel's birthday is truly a day to celebrate. His adoption has been a long journey and his first birthday with his new dad should be nothing less than memorable. It's a time to dismiss the battles and barriers between father and son and focus on the joy of our union. I greet my family and friends as they stream in around the many screaming children. Everyone, young and old, is in awe of the falling snow. Children run from the front to back yard, balling up little piles of dirty snowballs and heaving them at the unsuspecting adults standing nearby.

Friends and family alike are taken by Paulina's kindness and the genuine love she demonstrates so freely for my son and his playmates. She gathers the children in the backyard and joins them in creating a malnourished snowman from the quickly melting snow. Lemon seeds from my neighbors' tree become the eyes, a small pine cone is pushed in the middle of the face for a nose, Miguel places yellow pencils in the shape of a mouth, and my baseball cap lies gently across the miniature snowman's head. Children pose for photos as their parents cheer their snowy creation.

The kids are oblivious to the overwhelming damp and musty smell of the garage; gymnastics is a homerun with these energetic youngsters. Later, they laugh while slipping and sliding in the wet grass. For many, it's their first time playing tug-of-war. They trip and fall during the three-legged race. Paulina leads the group of exuberant children to the front yard to face Manny, the piñata, who now hangs from the lone tree. They line up from smallest to largest, and one at a time are blindfolded and set free to swing. One after the other, each child connects the plastic bat hard against the piñata but not one is able to break it open. They grow anxious awaiting the fall of the sugary treats. As the children begin chanting, "Candy, candy, candy…" Paulina pulls Manny's head off and spreads the contents throughout the yard. Children dive to the ground collecting the many pieces of candy. Miguel gathers treats for his half-brother Javier, who struggles to outmaneuver the larger children. Others shove smaller ones in an effort to hoard as much as possible. Throughout, Paulina remains vigilant, ensuring the smallest among the rowdy group have an equal amount. Then the parents and children retreat to the backyard for more planned activities. I approach Paulina.

"You're a guest." We've talked about this very topic several times over the last week. I remind her of our earlier conversations. But she'll have no part of it, and smiles as she continues picking up pieces of the broken piñata.

"It's not fair," one of my friends says near the end of the party. Over the last six months he's heard me talk often about Paulina. "You have had it too easy, too soon, and it really needs to come to an end." We laugh as we watch Paulina, who is now busy picking up plates and cups. *"No mas, Paulina,"* I shout. *"Descansa,"* I implore her to stop. My friend tells me he's tried to convince his wife to hire someone to care for their two boys in their own home. The children spend long days in childcare as he and his wife work more than full-time. His wife worries about a stranger caring for her two young sons. He likes the boys' preschool but he wants more of what he sees from Paulina. "You're lucky to have found her," he says on his way out the front door. "Let me know if she has a sister."

I collapse in an oversized chair as the last guests leave; Paulina sits on the small loveseat next to me. She puts her feet on the coffee table and rests her hands behind her head. She sighs loudly and we both laugh. We're dead to the world but content with our efforts. My feet are screaming as I lift them on top of the ottoman. "*Tu familia y amigos son muy amables*," she says my family and friends are kind. "*Extraño a mi familia*." It's been more than a year since she has seen her parents and siblings and she misses them. We sit quietly.

As we rest, I see Miguel through the sliding glass door. The snow has melted and the presents are unwrapped and sit in a reckless pile on the patio. Miguel intently hammers nails into wood on his new workbench, a gift from his grandpa. Of all the toys, Miguel gravitates to this one. In every way, he is Grandpa's boy. But there's more to it. At age four, Miguel shows an amazing mechanical talent. He yearns to use his hands to fix and repair. He's only at peace when his mind is fully engaged through his hands. Miguel is overflowing with pride as he jumps up and down and waves his wooden creation. In all of his complexity, through all his anger and rage, it is in this moment that I finally understand that everything will be okay. My overwhelming fears of his future soften. He has much to overcome, yet in this moment, he has so much to offer the world. I am certain his road won't be easy. The neglect and mistreatment from his earliest years can never be erased, but slowly he is evolving. There's no meltdown to report from today's party and that is progress. Through days filled with both hope and helplessness, I persevere. Not unlike my own father, I feel unequipped to handle this little boy and his immense needs, but I am fully committed to do my best. My son is a survivor and I owe him this much.

If nothing else, I am learning, but the lessons don't come easy. My son has immediate needs and demands my full attention. As a parent, especially a single parent, there are few timeouts. Plain and simple, I have learned to suck it up. The show must go on. More than ever, I feel blessed to have Paulina in my life. We serve as a collective voice of reason – a firm boundary that provides a stable and solid wall of love. Daily, Miguel fights authority and structure, but without it he would surely flounder and perish.

I am learning that all works out in the end. A little snow and a damp garage at the end of the day did nothing to stop an energetic group of small children from having a great time. In fact, the unexpected only made the day more memorable.

Most profound, Paulina's arrival into our household is nothing less than an act of divine intervention. Without her presence, I would be lost. She has taught me to recognize Miguel's true talents rather than be consumed by his deficits.

I awake to a distant sound of hammering. Paulina is now up and washing dishes. I stumble to the garage and realize my dad has returned with a new hot water heater and is installing it. Not unlike when I was Miguel's age, I dutifully hold the flashlight. "Miguel, turn the wrench over and over," my dad says gently to his grandson. "Grandpa, this way? Does it go this way?" Miguel clarifies as he turns the wrench clockwise. "You are such a big boy," my dad says proudly, "...and so smart." I desperately need my dad, not to mention how much my son needs him as well. He shares something so inherent with Miguel that I know the two are made for one another. He will forever have a prominent place in my son's heart.

"It's gonna take some time for your old man," my father says as I walk him to his truck, his arm around my shoulder. The man before me is filled with visible emotion and demonstrative affection that I've never seen. My son has the combination to a lock which sets his vulnerability free. "I am so proud of you, son, for what you are doing for that little guy. He's a lucky kid." He rolls up his window and drives away before the moment overcomes the two of us.

A week after the party, I am in Palm Springs on business. My mom stops by the house to see Paulina and Miguel. Paulina presents her with a pile of note cards with Spanish words on one side and the English translation on the other.

"I can't wait to try them out," my mom says excitedly over the phone. "You watch, I'll get your father to practice with me too."

TEN

Unjust Goodbye

I have become oblivious to the yellow Post-it Notes that are everywhere and are a fixture in our house, like a piece of artwork that hangs eternally in the same spot undetected among the interior landscape. "La Lavadora de Platos"—reads the dishwasher; "El Horno"—the oven; "La Silla" – the overstuffed armchair. Paulina has taken my challenge to heart. The usefulness of these yellow squares has long since passed and they now dot the tile and carpet. As they lose their grip, one by one, I tape them to extend their purposeful mission. It's become part of my daily routine. I think nothing of it.

The Post-it Notes are part of an elaborate game of hide and seek, Miguel's favorite. Paulina adds her own twist that captures my son's attention and reinforces his Spanish. She directs Miguel to close his eyes as she quietly hides items. I laugh as she tiptoes through the house with appliances big and small tucked under her arms. Miguel's Mickey Mouse stopwatch hangs from her neck. Her large size makes this all the more comical. Her limitless creativity is directed entirely at my son. She is fully in her element; who else could produce such fun?

When all items are securely hidden, the game begins. "*Miguel, donde esta la tostadora?*" she asks as she activates the stopwatch. He quickly realizes he is to find the toaster. He's clear on his mission as he races around the house with uncontrolled determination, the stopwatch always present on his mind. He runs to the kitchen, but the toaster is nowhere to be found. That would be too easy. Not in the magic hall closet, and not in the garage either. "I can find it. I can find it. Don't tell me. You better not tell me!" Miguel yells from the back of the house. Not under the bathroom sink; too big to fit under the couch. Why of course, under his dad's pillow! Sporting a huge smile, he races back to the living room with toaster in hand, a large pile of crumbs left behind. "Forty-five seconds," Paulina yells out as Miguel presents the toaster before her. He is rewarded with hugs and *Conchas,* big shell-like sweet rolls.

Miguel is learning Spanish, but I am learning many valuable lessons as well. Paulina has an amazing ability to captivate and entertain my son. Over the last nine months, she's taught me much, but nothing more valuable than to slow down and treasure these simple moments. I'm finally learning to focus less on the number of activities in any given day and instead on the quality of them. I give thanks for the good times and work hard not to obsess over the unanswered questions regarding the future.

With Paulina's help, I've come to better understand myself and the commitment I've made to my son. Without a partner or spouse standing by, it's easy to second-guess yourself. It has taken almost a year, but I finally get it. My pledge to Miguel is not a test run. Parenting provides no money-back guarantees, and any applicable warranties have long since expired. There are no exit strategies. Unconditional love remains the lesson, repeated day in and day out. Although Miguel thrives on creating chaos and anarchy in an effort to overturn the very structure and authority he craves, I'm slowly gaining the upper hand. With the help of Paulina, I better understand Miguel's hurt and his resulting motivations. I watch her like a hawk. On the darkest and most difficult days, her compassion and resilience are nothing short of courageous. Unlike my own inclination to exert authority and power to subdue and restore order, she finds a different, more compassionate approach. Paulina understands that Miguel's anger is an integral part of his personality. Wounds inflicted upon young children create a pain that is raw and powerful, and that can lead to unforeseen fury, which can be spontaneous and vicious. Oftentimes there is little rhyme or reason for such violent outbursts. The fallout takes its toll on those who love these children the most. No one remains unscathed.

Hours earlier, before the game of hide and seek, I found Paulina sitting behind a closed door on the corner of the bed in the spare bedroom. When all else fails, this is her retreat from my son's uncontrolled rage. The blinds were closed and it was dark. She was weeping. Her sadness filled the small bedroom; her sorrow was heartbreaking. "He's a good boy," she said, embarrassed by her tears. In true selfless fashion, she was concerned that I would think less of Miguel. She took her large t-shirt and wiped her eyes dry. "He wanted sprinkles for the cookies," she said.

When Paulina refused his many pleas to go to the store and buy them, Miguel erupted in anger. She suggested topping the cookies with melted chocolate, but Miguel wanted what he wanted. As she attempted to ignore his outburst, he took the hot cookie sheets and threw them against the kitchen cabinets. Cookies dispersed everywhere. "I hate you!" he screamed for the first time at Paulina. "I hate you!" He ran from the kitchen in a rage, his hands scalded and burned from the heat of the metal trays. She had heard Miguel yell these words at his father many times, but he'd never directed them so explicitly at her.

After Paulina cleaned up the mess in the kitchen and stacked the cookies neatly on the ceramic serving dish, she retreated to the safety of the small room and wept. Miguel had since fallen asleep, exhausted from his outburst. "Paulina, he loves you," I said as I sat on the bed with her. I believed this with all my heart. "He loves you so much." I felt compelled to tell her this although it was obvious to any stranger's eye. "*Yo sé,*" she said, but there was no escaping the hurt. "*Sí,*" she whispered.

Over the last nine months, I have grown closer to Paulina than my own family. She sees what few others see when darkness erupts into violence, and understands my times of helplessness. When I am ready to quit, she is the one who pulls me back up on my feet to face another round. I gain strength from her presence.

At that moment, other than my son, there was no one more important in my life. "How about a cookie?" I jabbed her in the side as we both laughed and headed to the kitchen.

A week later, on a rare rainy Phoenix night, I linger, actually loiter, outside in a light sprinkle, watching Paulina and my son at the dining room table. I peer through the window by the front door. On the table sit animal picture cards labeled in Spanish. Paulina imitates animals as Miguel guesses them, yelling the names out in Spanish. My favorite is Paulina as both matador and bull. Thinking back now, the game was not nearly as important as my conclusions from the evening. The thought that I could give my son all he needed was unrealistic and selfish. Paulina brought something to the equation at which I could only marvel. She was content in every moment. There was no distraction that pulled her anywhere but closer to my son. Paulina, well-versed in her role as my son's nanny, was likely unaware of the important lessons she had imparted on me as a new father.

Immediately, I know something is wrong as I walk through the front door; it's written all over her face. This night is to be one of our last. Skipping the usual rundown on the evening's events, Paulina shies away, refusing to look me in the eye.

She quickly ushers Miguel down the hallway and begins preparing him for bedtime. Anxious, I keep myself preoccupied. I'm nervous, unwilling to face what I fear she will tell me. I shuffle through the mail and remove the clean dishes from the dishwasher. I pick up Miguel's toys and clean up the remains of an earlier art project. I'm uneasy and anxious because I know in my heart she is irreplaceable. In some unconventional way, we have become soul mates.

I cannot do this without her; there remains so much more to do and our achievements have only come through a team effort. Paulina deserves much of the credit. She's the one who redirected the fledgling yet failing game plan. Left to my own devices I would have bullied my way to defeat. She's the one who consistently doled out compassion versus control. So many times, she was the coach, and I her trusted assistant. I can't imagine the last year without her.

Miguel stands before me, his teeth brushed and pajamas on. He's ready for bed and happy. I feel hopeful suddenly, and my optimism overshadows worry or fear. This alone is newsworthy. The front page headline is clear: My son is happy.

Paulina hands off Miguel and quickly heads to the kitchen. In his small hand, he holds, *Babar*, his favorite book. I pick up my son and place him in bed. He smells clean as I inch my way next to him. Of all his books, Miguel loves the story of *Babar*. It's clearly meaningful; he relates to the little elephant who becomes an orphan after his mother is shot by poachers. Babar leaves his village as a young cub and wanders to a strange town, befriended by an elderly woman. Single-handedly, she houses, feeds, and loves him. Later, fully grown, Babar returns to his village and marries his childhood sweetheart and becomes king. Thankfully, on this night, Miguel quickly falls asleep before the poachers come for Babar's mother.

As I look at my little boy peacefully sleeping, I feel the world is filled with endless possibilities. This child, who has come from such tumultuous beginnings, has made monumental progress. I kiss him softly and whisper, "I am a lucky guy!"

Paulina sits uneasily on the couch, tears streaming down her face. A pit in my stomach forms as she begins to speak. "*Necesito regresar a México,*" she says. "*Mi mamá no está bien.*" Her mom is sick and she must return to Mexico. There is no avoiding the impending goodbye. Over the next thirty minutes, through tears, she tells me more about her life than we've shared with each other over the last nine months. Paulina confides that she and Sergio are in the country illegally. She's scared, and at some level has been since arriving in Phoenix. She fears being incarcerated and deported. They entered the country on travel visas more than a year ago and have overstayed their welcome. The documents she provided me are her cousin's. She says that Sergio has lied at work as well. All this time he has been known as Arturo, the name matching the one on his fraudulent social security card.

The constant fear of living in the country has taken its toll. "I'm not a criminal, I'm not a bad person," she repeats through her tears. Now, with her mother sick, it all has become too much. The decision is clear but not easy. Sergio and Paulina will return immediately. They'll move into a small apartment back in Monterey, Mexico, near her ailing mother and remaining siblings. They have nothing tangible to show for their time in the United States. Indeed, her long list of unfulfilled dreams—including one day becoming an artist and her aspirations for higher education—now seem a fleeting desire. What kind of life awaits the two of them back in Mexico? And what will become of Paulina's dreams?

There is more she wants to share as she thanks me for our time together. "I will never have children," Paulina sobs in hysterics. She and Sergio have been trying for years but doctors have confirmed that their only real choice is adoption. The cost of medical procedures and adoption will deprive her of motherhood, an impossible reality for a woman who is irrepressible.

"Juan, do you think I would make a good mother?" she asks in Spanish in a quiet voice, a continued stream of tears running down her round cheeks. "*Absolutamente,*" I repeat over and over.

My thoughts race back to our first night together, Paulina lifting Miguel up on her chest and rocking him to sleep, her singing soft and sweet. The endless love for my little boy, her unlimited creativity and heroic patience, now go unrealized, her dreams punctured and beaten down. Is there someone more deserving of a child than Paulina? I can think of no other. This night, few things, if any, seem less just in this world.

Our final night together, Paulina avoids dwelling on her imminent departure. For one more night, she remains the closest thing to a mother Miguel has known. The memory of his own birth mother has long been erased as well as the fond memories of Ramona, his foster mother. Paulina's only wish is that this final night be like all others. She wants to remember it as joyful and not consumed by sadness. As a result, we're diligent in following the nightly routine. She and Miguel make tacos one final time. The three of us load the dishwasher as we have so many nights before. After dinner, we walk to the desert to feed the birds and chase the rabbits. Miguel sits in his wagon as we pull him up the gentle sloping street. Paulina hugs Stephanie the bird lady as they say goodbye. The birds and rabbits linger long after the food is gone, as if they too know this will be the last time they'll see the large, funny woman from Mexico. As we begin to leave, Paulina turns one last time and looks at the desert. The multitude of cactus and plants are now in full bloom. She sees the beauty beyond the rough exterior of the harsh dry desert. Colors are everywhere; they're inescapable. "*Es muy bonito, Juan, muy bonito,*" she says wistfully. She is overwhelmed by the simplicity of the moment. Fortunately, the finality of it all escapes my small son. "When are you coming back?" Miguel again asks from his perch in the wagon. "She is not coming back, son." I gently remind him. "Paulina's mom is sick and she needs to go and take care of her."

She prepares Miguel for bed one final time. They sing her funny monkey song as he brushes his teeth. She picks him up and gently rocks him to sleep. I watch from down the hall as she gently strokes his hair to calm him. He's now several pounds heavier, yet she remains unfazed. Miguel doesn't fight sleep; he surrenders quickly. They are, as ever, a perfect fit.

ELEVEN

The Square

My friends are right. I am spoiled and now I feel lost. Paulina's been gone less than a week and I miss my confidante and companion. I miss everything about her, but most of all I miss her largeness. She filled the house and I never felt alone. Now, it feels empty, but nowhere more so than the kitchen, which was once the center of all activity. I pass through quickly to avoid the painful waves of isolation. Miguel and I gravitate to the family room where we eat dinner in front of the T.V. rather than sit, as we always have, at the barstools around the kitchen counter. I can't bear looking at the emptiness of that space; our voices echo off the outdated dark brown walnut cabinets. We struggle to ignore our missing link.

I know it's time to move on and yet I linger, not ready to let go. "When is she coming back?" Miguel asks daily. I do my best to assure him that we're looking for another Paulina, knowing full well there is no such person. Like him, I feel unsettled since her swift departure. Overnight, my sounding board vanished. Only she knew my uncertainties and fears. Only Paulina knew the complexities of my son and the delicate tightrope we walk. Her size and compassion were my safety net. Restless and unable to sleep, at times I feel I am free falling.

Early Saturday morning the phone rings. A woman named Maria calls after seeing my ad in the morning paper. It's almost identical to the one that I placed less than a year ago. She is a grandmother who is raising her teenage son and sounds eager to work. I am a veteran of the search process and as a result, this time around my game plan will be different. I'm committed to interviewing several women and thoroughly checking their references, but I am once again in a bind. My job is requiring more late night meetings and evening events that I must attend and I need help fast. I won't let my emotions overcome logic; I won't jump at the first viable candidate despite being under the gun. As I weed through the variety of women, some dysfunctional and others desperate in their search for work, I know this task will be difficult.

Maria insists on calling me "Mr. John" throughout our short phone conversation. She says she loves children and that she's just completed work with another family. She's flexible to watch Miguel in our house or care for him in her own. "Mr. John, whatever you need I can do. I won't disappoint you." She sounds caring and kind, but most importantly she sounds normal. She's fluent in both English and Spanish, nimbly bouncing between the two languages. She assures me she has references and the fact that she lives close by is a plus. We agree to meet for an interview. I repeat several times that this is just an initial visit; a meet and greet.

I wake up Miguel and make him pancakes just the way Paulina did. "The middle is gooey," Miguel complains. He's right; we both miss her cooking. Before hitting the road, we eat Frosted Flakes. I am relieved he has forgotten the horrid meltdown from the night before. He's been agitated and upset since Paulina's departure.

I circle the same block of dilapidated mobile homes searching for Maria's address. After our second lap, I realize we're in "the square," an informal designation created by the Phoenix Police Department. This piecemeal neighborhood has some of the highest crime per square mile in Phoenix. Drugs fuel much of the problem. An expressway and new sound barriers conveniently disguise the rundown collection of trailers and apartment complexes. Morning commuters unknowingly pass the abundance of illegal activity just beyond the large cement walls. Other than the residents who call this neighborhood home, and those dropping in to score a quick hit, there are few other reasons to pass through this area. As we search for Maria's house, there are several young men in baggy pants and "wife-beater" t-shirts engaged in negotiation. They hover around a black Monte Carlo low-rider. A Hispanic teenager in long shorts and knee high sport socks runs away from the group and down an alley as the low-rider speeds off. It all happens very fast. I look back at Miguel in the rearview mirror; he is quiet but observant of all that's unfolding.

One rundown trailer after the other lines Stewart Street. Many of the trailers have additional wood structures that have been haphazardly pasted to them to expand the tiny living space within. The expanse of metal structures is a snapshot from a third world country. I fail to find Maria's street address. Again, I circle the block, and discover more broken down cars and uncontrolled weeds littering most front yards. We pass a silver Winnebago travel trailer wedged between the carport of a faded blue double-wide mobile home and an adjacent brightly painted gold single wide trailer. A middle-aged couple sits just outside the silver Winnebago in burnt orange recliners, weeds growing around them. The man is Hispanic and his face heavily pitted. He wears only oil-stained jeans, with no shirt or shoes. His companion is Caucasian. Her hair stands wild with bleached blond streaks that are overwhelmed by dark roots. Life hasn't been kind. She wears tight terry-cloth shorts, a "wife-beater" and flip-flops. As our car slowly approaches, they light cigarettes and stare intently.

"*Donde vive María?*" I ask the man if he knows where Maria lives. "*Allá!*" The man points to the end of the block; he is clearly high on something. As I roll up my window, a small girl runs out of the trailer in her underpants, with no t-shirt, just in time to see us drive away.

Maria sits on a bench in front of her trailer. She is in her late fifties; her salt and pepper hair is braided and pulled tight. Smiling, she stands and waves me up the driveway. Her teeth are brown and visibly rotten. She has a dark complexion and looks Mayan, like many of the indigenous people of Mexico and Central America. She hugs me as I walk up to greet her.

"You found me," she says. "Nice to meet you," I reply taking in my surroundings. An ancient Chevy Citation rests snugly in the carport, surrounded by tall stacks of tires and rusted car parts. Her front yard is tiny and barren, with a handful of flowering weeds that brighten an otherwise dismal view.

She drops to one knee. "You must be Miguel." She is nose to nose with him as she hugs him tightly. "Yep," Miguel responds, unconcerned about his surroundings. Maria is sweet and gentle. She puts her arm around me as I help her up. She directs me to several steps that lead into her trailer and groans slightly as she makes her way up the flight of wooden stairs. It's dark and musty inside and the curtains are pulled closed over each of the small windows. I conceal my concern with an overcompensating game show smile. We sit at the small kitchen table which has four chairs but only room for three to sit comfortably. She turns the kitchen light on; sunshine begs to infiltrate this small space.

Down the dark narrow hallway, a door swings open. Hidden behind a mop of black hair, a lanky teenager mutters something as he slams the front door on his way out. Maria frowns as she shares that her grandson is living with her until the boy's mother can steer clear of jail and a persistent drug problem.

As she speaks, I actively create an exit strategy. The vivid details of Maria's life story are heartbreaking. Her husband died more than fifteen years ago from a heart attack. "It's just me," she says. Her daughter's drug addiction has cost her most everything. Asthma and an irregular heartbeat have been consistent health burdens, not to mention the rebellious grandson. Her extended family has all but abandoned her. "It's just me," she says again. "Maria is the only one left to take care of Maria." She receives disability payments from the government, yet works as a babysitter, always paid under the table to make ends meet.

Maria encourages Miguel to play outside; however, I keep a firm grip on both his hands as he sits on my lap. From my vantage point, I can see the couple who I encountered further down the street, and don't trust the immediate surroundings. After fifteen minutes, my cell phone rings; it's my mother calling, which serves as our ticket out. Abruptly I explain to Maria that we're overdue at Miguel's grandmother's house for breakfast. She can't hide her desperation and senses things are not going well. I stand to go as she pleads for a single chance to babysit. She's certain that if I see her in action it will dispel any of my concerns. "I can work any time, any time you need," she begins to cry as I buckle Miguel into his car seat. "How about you try me tonight?" She sounds distraught.

"I'll take good care of him," she says as she kisses Miguel through the open car window. "I will be in touch," I say, blatantly lying to her as I roll up the window. Prior to backing out of the driveway, I lock the doors and windows. The couple near the Winnebago watches our departure closely. I wave at them awkwardly and quickly drive away.

Five messages await our return—four from women and one man calling for his Spanish speaking mother. They leave messages, several in Spanish, inquiring about the job. I write down their names and contact information on a large yellow legal pad that will be filled by week's end. I set the pad aside and suggest to Miguel we go swimming. After our visit with Maria, I'm not ready.

TWELVE

Unlikely Missionary

I first meet Carmen at her son's house. Rodrigo is tall and bulky and extends his chunky hand to greet me. He drives a jacked-up new pick-up truck that makes it difficult for anyone other than himself to get in and out. He's polite but quiet. Carmen lives with her son, his wife, and their two children in a modest but well-kept neighborhood in West Phoenix. Rodrigo encourages his son Hector to play with Miguel in the front yard; the two boys throw a football back and forth under a spotlight that Rodrigo has rigged up to extend daylight.

Carmen is surrounded by her son and his family. They are friendly and appear to love one another deeply. This immediately feels like what I'm looking for. We speak English, although Carmen defaults to Spanish when she wants to ensure she is understood. When necessary, her son repeats the message in English. Carmen's granddaughter, Silvia, remains firmly attached to her knee for our entire meeting. She gently combs and braids the little girl's hair as she answers each of my questions. In passing, Carmen mentions she is Mormon and casually reveals that she is in the country illegally. She hopes to gain citizenship through her son, but this will take several years.

"Can you smell it?" he asks. The small house smells like disinfectant; Carmen smiles proudly. "She loves to clean," Rodrigo says of his mother.

I feel anxious during the interview. Since my visit to Maria, I've interviewed about a dozen candidates over the phone and met four in their homes; I've yet to find an appropriate match. I feel good about Carmen and her family, but it's clear her interest in working is more about a paycheck than a vocation. The tone is that of a traditional job interview. Carmen asks many questions about when and how she will get paid. After some brief discussion I agree, if she is hired, to pay her every Friday, in cash rather than a check. "Do you pay on time?" she asks abruptly in English. Rodrigo makes an effort to soften his mother's stern demeanor. He explains that other families have not paid her for her work, taking advantage of her. All this talk of payment and logistics pulls me back to Paulina. However, I must move on. I'm running out of time and need help. This is my circumstance and I need to face it. I can no longer juggle my work and Miguel's schedule without assistance. Almost a month has passed since Paulina left us.

Pending a reference check, I offer Carmen the job and she indicates she can start on Monday. Over the weekend, I call several people from her church, including a mother who employed her. The feedback is positive, which helps me set aside any reservations. "I wish I could have her back," the mother tells me. Her husband's business has slowed and they can no longer afford to pay a babysitter.

Over the last month, Miguel has appeared lonely and especially irritable. This seems only natural, given how close he'd been to Paulina. We both grieve the loss in our own way. I find I'm less willing to plunk down with Miguel and play without Paulina close by. What would she do in this situation or that? I often wonder. I find it a challenge to satisfy my son's insatiable imagination and creativity. He has a million ideas that must be acted upon, and often gets frustrated when I have no suggestion for how to better his many inventions. I fight to stay in the moment as Paulina did so effortlessly. Her replacement cannot start soon enough.

Miguel is excited about Carmen's arrival, but soon after her first visit he wanders from room to room searching for some spontaneous project to fill his time. He's forgotten how to play and entertain himself and looks to Carmen to save the day. Yet she is more an observer than participant. Where Paulina was down on the floor with Miguel building Lincoln Logs and Legos, Carmen prefers to sit on the couch and support Miguel from a comfortable distance. She's more subdued cheerleader than compatriot. Given her age and tempered personality, I find it hard to direct her to engage with more enthusiasm.

For Carmen's second visit, Miguel is in full meltdown mode. He wakes on the wrong side of the bed, looking to spark a dispute. Still angry at me for not letting him watch a second video the night before, he refused to brush his teeth or put his pajamas on, and I sent him to his room. He threw several books at me when I attempted to read him a story before bed, leaving his room a mess, and his small bookcase disassembled and covering the floor. He spent an hour screaming before he fell asleep on the carpet at the foot of his bed.

This regression is happening more and more since Paulina's departure. Miguel does not do well with transition and instead of embracing those who love him during these times of upheaval, he becomes even more angry and defiant at them. My biggest concern is these outbursts may startle our new babysitter and send her running.

Upon Carmen's arrival, he's in battle mode. She goes into his room, where he sits in the corner with his well-seasoned scowl plastered across his small face. He half-heartedly throws a stuffed animal at her and screams, "NO!" Carmen will have none of the pouting and holds up large cookies she's brought for him. "*Ven a la cocina. Tengo galletas.*" She directs him to meet her in the kitchen, and then closes the door. I leave soon after and she tells me later that Miguel came right out after hearing me leave. He's hungry and eats three cookies and afterwards helps her clean up his room, somehow managing to reconstruct the bookshelf and stack his books back on top of it. Upon my return, he's rebounded and is once again happy after twenty hours of turmoil.

Miguel is persistent in wanting a playmate in his new nanny. He appears confused and at times gets annoyed at his caregiver. While I can't criticize Carmen for not being Paulina, if I'm to be honest, I am disappointed. Nonetheless, Miguel is safe and cared for and a relative calm has returned to our household. And most importantly, Carmen is confident and doesn't appear to scare easily.

Carmen's sense of order is a welcome addition, as is the smell of cleanliness. Lysol aroma permeates the house. In short order she has reorganized the kitchen cabinets and pantry. Over protests from Miguel, she's cleaned the shelves in the garage and de-cluttered the infamous magic hall closet. She has rearranged clothing, neatly refolding shirts and underwear in each of our dressers, and sanitized most everything in the house. I become intoxicated by the smell of disinfectant.

Although I talk of Miguel's recent baptism and attending Mass on Sundays, Carmen regularly leaves Latter Day Saints pamphlets in a variety of locations throughout our house. She strategically positions them next to the computer, near the phone, or on the dining room table. *The Prophet's Testimony* I find among the magazines in the bathroom. Another, *The Purpose of Life*, is left on the coffee table, under the television remote. The pamphlets feature happy families, a smiling mother and father, and a brood of gleeful children. Carmen writes impassioned notes, an invitation for us to join her and her family in the Mormon way.

"Carmen, gracias por los panfletos, pero somos Católicos," I repeat on numerous occasions over the last two months. These reminders about our Catholic faith don't dampen her commitment to her apparent mission of conversion. As more of a game than a personal calling, I begin leaving my own faith favors to be discovered. I pull the large box of family photos from the top shelf of the coat closet and search through the photos of Miguel's baptism and the family

party that followed. In one, Miguel and I stand next to our parish priest in full vestments; the baptismal font sits close to our side. I leave the photos on the kitchen counter, and on the back write "Miguel's Baptism." I select several others with his godparents and one with the two of us pictured in front of the altar. I place these on the refrigerator and on my nightstand. Later in the week, I notice Carmen has moved all of these photos to the top of the pile of mail.

Once again I read about Joseph Smith, Jr. and his discovery of the Golden Tablets, as well as the early formation of his Church of Latter-day Saints. Carmen has graduated from pamphlets to full-blown chronicles that capture the history of the church from its very beginnings to the present movement. Left on my nightstand, this particular book has a short inscription handwritten in Spanish; it seeks our conversion. Our newest nanny appears to be on the mission of a lifetime. "Would you like to attend church with my family?" she doggedly asks. I try not to compare her to Paulina, but it's impossible. As I desperately struggle to establish common ground, I feel like our home has become an exchange program for foreign missionaries. "You need to give her a chance," my mom coaches me. "There's only one Paulina."

"I didn't know you Mormons were so popular in Mexico," I kid with a close work friend. He's Mormon and Mexican American. "What do you think I was doing in Mexico for two years before I went to college? Did you think I was on a Club Med vacation?" He laughs at my disbelief. Although, I see young men riding their bikes on the streets throughout Phoenix with their white shirts and ties, I'm still taken by the large presence of Mormons in Mexico. I go online and learn that Mormons and Evangelical Christians are two of the fastest growing denominations south of the U.S. border.

Repetition brings a sense of calm. Over the next three months, routine quickly settles in. Out of necessity, Miguel has learned to be more independent in his playtime. Returning from the gym early Saturday morning, I watch him from the large picture window just outside our front door. He has moved our oversized sectional to the sides of the living room so that he can build one of his large

Lego castles. With the furniture out of the way, he can more easily survey his entire kingdom without interference. In addition to the Legos, he has introduced a pile of race cars and several small space ships. I watch him talk to himself as he snaps piece after piece on to the growing fortress. At times he gets frustrated and pulls the structure completely apart, but then reevaluates his options and creates a large fort. Carmen walks through the room and pats him on the head as she carries a full basket of laundry, and then again minutes later she reappears with clean sheets to make up beds. I stay put – watching, secretly hoping to find fault with my new nanny. She comes into view a third time and stops to comment on Miguel's growing kingdom, which brings a smile to his face. She's back a fourth time with a mop and bucket and headed to the hall bathroom; she's on a cleaning frenzy. Again, she says something to him that makes him smile. I can't hear the words but there is no mistaking this woman's intent: she acts from love. I've created an impossible standard and now it's time to let go of the past. I need to stop the comparisons. I feel guilty for spying on the two of them, but it helps me reach a turning point. Carmen loves my son and she is dutiful in her work. I can't ask for more. Miguel is once again happy.

It's been weeks in the making but tonight I finally convince Carmen to let me and Miguel help prepare dinner. She's taken to cooking one big meal a week, and then leaving the leftovers in the refrigerator for dinner on other nights. She's uneasy with the idea of men in her kitchen, but allows us in. Resigned, she directs Miguel to grate cheese while I am handed a knife and cutting board. I begin dicing tomatoes. She sautés chicken, all the while keeping a watchful eye on the two of us. As quickly as Miguel can grate a small pile, he fills his mouth with a handful of cheese. I join Miguel in sampling the small piles of preparations. "*No más,*" Carmen says laughing and pointing her fingers at each of us. "*No más antes de la cena.*" She's worried that we are doing more eating than cooking and warns there will be no remaining food for dinner. After a long absence, laughter is welcome. She puts the cooked chicken, tomatoes, beans, spices, and cheese into a pan and allows Miguel to crack an egg into a bowl of batter, which will soon be cornbread. Shells from the egg litter the bowl. Carmen picks out the shells and demonstrates to Miguel how to break the egg gently so the shell stays intact. He watches with awe as his nanny cracks the second egg effortlessly. Miguel breaks the third egg successfully and Carmen cheers for her little helper and kisses him on the forehead. She seems to be warming to her new extended family. This meal has transformed her from task master to grandmother. She allows Miguel to spread the cornbread batter over the contents. He hesitates, thinking the batter should go in a separate container. "No *mijo*, trust me, trust me. It will work." Teaching men how to cook is a new experience, but Carmen is clearly enjoying herself.

While the Mexican casserole bakes, we get busy on dessert. She's brought a box of brownie mix and hands it to Miguel with a smile. "It's your turn." He looks at me for direction but I point back to Carmen. *"Ella es tu maestra"*—I say his nanny is now his teacher, not his dad. She tells him what is needed. He pulls out a pan and places two large wooden spoons in either of his back pockets. He takes the carton of eggs from the refrigerator; he can barely contain his excitement knowing he'll get to crack two more. He finds the measuring cup and fills it partially with water and pours it into the brown powdery mix. In no time, the contents are emptied into the pan and placed in the oven. Miguel gets busy eating the remaining mix from the bowl with his big wooden spoon. Chocolate batter is smeared all over his face.

Tonight, Carmen joins us for dinner, something she hasn't yet done. Miguel and I eat like there's no tomorrow. Somehow the food tastes better knowing that we had a hand in creating it. I load the dishwasher and wash the larger bowls that won't fit. It gets dark out and I see the reflection of Carmen and Miguel behind me through the large kitchen window; I feel like I'm watching a drive-in movie. Miguel works side by side with his nanny to find the right size plastic containers to store the leftovers. In our house, this is no small task. Soon the counter is filled with plastic. Through the reflection, I see a softer side of Carmen. Somehow this evening, Miguel has transformed into another grandchild. She uses the same soft tone in her voice that I first heard when she talked with her granddaughter, Sylvia. As the night comes to the end, Carmen volunteers to put Miguel to bed. She lies near his side and I hear her sing softly. Fifteen minutes later, I find both are sound asleep on the small single bed. Soon after, her son, Rodrigo, appears at the door and I gently wake her. She's slightly embarrassed. "*Gracias por todo*," I say as I hug her for the first time, thanking her for all her efforts.

It's several weeks later when I return home from work to find Carmen reading a picture book to Miguel about the early Mormon migration to Utah. I sit on the couch and listen as she reads in Spanish about persecution of early church members. She's filled with emotion and animation; she's an energetic and impassioned storyteller. She reads of the early pioneer church members, forging their way through mountains and streams as they eventually settle in Utah. Miguel is captivated by the pictures of wagon trains heading westward. Once the Mormon pioneers reach their promised land, they are pictured pointing to a valley far below. As she closes the book, Carmen smiles. She looks inspired and fulfilled to have an audience of potential converts.

Soon after, Carmen informs me that she must leave early. Her son is picking her up to attend church. Later, on the nightstand, a Mormon bible awaits; another heartfelt inscription is handwritten on the inside cover. I decide that I need to talk with her once again about her missionary fervor and explain that although the world is her oyster, the population of potential converts exists outside the bounds of our home.

On Saturday morning, Carmen looks serious. I'm set to initiate our discussion on religious freedom, but before I have a chance, she asks if we can talk alone on the patio. Immediately, I recognize the somber tone. She'll be leaving us. With just six months service, there's little emotion as she tells me about her future plans. Shell-shocked, I miss much of what she shares as I realize I'll soon be faced with finding another nanny and the resulting transition. As Carmen tells me of her plans to move to Ogden, Utah, a suburb outside Salt Lake City, I'm distracted by the clothesline that sits just behind her. I zone in and out of the conversation, lost in fond memories of the many art projects from Miguel and Paulina that were once pinned along the line. Carmen is excited and uncharacteristically animated about her impending move, explaining that she'll be closer to her church and her faith. She's filled with the same passion I saw when she read the Mormon children's book to Miguel.

I understand this is a necessary journey; she is a woman with unlimited faith and her devotion is undeniable. Although she has few material possessions, she's finally pursuing her calling. "*Buena suerte,*" I wish her good luck as we begin the difficult talk of her departure. We inadvertently revert to a business tone about the logistics of her final days. Extracting the emotion from this conversation makes it easier for both of us.

I again become mired in memories of Paulina. I thought I'd moved beyond this point, but now from every viewpoint in the kitchen, she resurfaces. Front and center on the refrigerator, a beautiful picture of a flowering cactus remains. In her final days, Paulina presented this gift to Miguel. Since then, he won't let me remove the picture and replace it with the many drawings from school that regularly fill his miniature Spiderman backpack. Truthfully, I have had no interest in removing the many mementos spread throughout the house. The army of clay animal figurines still balance on the windowsill above the kitchen sink. Although they've lost their original shapes from their many falls into the soapy dishwater, there they stand. As I look out the kitchen window, the scarecrow is visible in the patch of weeds that once was the garden Miguel and Paulina tended. Taped firmly to the toaster is the yellow Post-it Note which reads, *La Tostadora*, the sole remaining vestige from our language lessons. I cling to these memories of Paulina and wonder: Did I really give Carmen a fair shake?

Carmen wants me to meet her friend, Ana, who she's convinced will be a good nanny and playmate for Miguel. "She's younger and has more energy, and she's Catholic," she says with a wink and a smile. Ana, the mother of two grown children, has recently separated from her husband. She plans to move to the United States to look for work as a nanny and will live with her daughter in Mesa, a suburb of Phoenix. Carmen clarifies that Ana has a travel visa and can legally live in the U.S. Though she's prohibited from working in the country, Ana won't face the daily fear of deportation like so many others from Mexico.

I've long since thrown away the list of potential nanny candidates who answered the last classified ad seven months earlier. Carmen has less than two weeks before she'll be on her way to her promised land. Early the following week, I agree to meet Ana. Every ounce of me hopes that she'll be exceptional and spare me a new round of interviews. Nonetheless, memories of Maria and her dimly lit trailer are inescapable.

Our last day with Carmen is surprisingly touching. She'll leave for Utah in the morning. Immediately she tears up when she sits down one final time with Miguel to say goodbye. "May the angels watch over you and protect you," she says in Spanish and then in English as she pins a small angel charm on his shirt. "You're a very good boy." She kisses his forehead, hugs me, and then disappears out the front door. Miguel and I watch her depart from our front window; she struggles to climb up into her son's large pick-up. Rodrigo runs around to help his mother into the towering vehicle. They drive away quickly.

THIRTEEN

Nanny Rebound

While eating dinner, Ana insists on standing at the counter. Just feet away, she's quiet and shy, unable to leave the security of the kitchen. We attempt to coax her into joining us at the retro turquoise colored banquette wedged snugly in the small breakfast nook. It's the inaugural meal in our new home and she's now part of our little family. It took Ana several weeks to wrap up unfinished business in Mexico, so this first day is especially sweet.

She's had a busy day. Ana is helping us move into our house and we're not alone. Two large Hispanic men from a moving company carry boxes and move much of the large furniture. Back and forth between the two houses, I shuttle carloads of fragile items. Ana and I take turns directing the men in Spanish.

Ana wastes no time, cleaning both the old and new houses before we break for lunch. In the afternoon, she unpacks dishes, meticulously organizing the kitchen and bathrooms. She arranges our clothing and makes up each of the beds. Miguel is her trusted assistant and trails closely behind. He's uncharacteristically sweet and reminds me of our earliest days together. She distracts him until we can locate his precious treasures that are spread throughout the house in several unidentified boxes. She came to us with one small suitcase of her own, which she quickly unpacks, arranging a handful of family photos equally split between a dresser and single nightstand.

Our new home is just blocks away, but separated by a busy main corridor. We're moving so that Miguel can attend a better public school. A larger mortgage payment and additional expenses will offset private school tuition. The neighborhood is a throwback; houses sit on oversized lots with grassy front yards, while children play ball and run through sprinklers with their friends. Our new home is also larger. It has a fourth bedroom to accommodate our nanny, who will be living with us during the week; she'll stay with her daughter on weekends. Her bedroom is off the kitchen and has a separate entrance that allows her to come and go when she wants. Extra space will come in handy. In addition to Ana's arrival, I receive news that Oscar, a three-year old Guatemalan boy living in an orphanage outside Guatemala City, will likely join our family. If all goes well, I'll visit the orphanage in six months and finalize an adoption within the year.

Only a fool would not second guess my decision to adopt again. For over a year, I've been in the middle of a tsunami that has shaken my foundation and upended all I've known to be true. I've been humbled by my young son and often reduced to tears in search of answers from my maker. The subtext of these prayers is a plea for clarity, a simple solution for an incredibly complex child. In the end, the answer is neither clear nor simple, but rather steady—a routine and repetition filled with unconditional love. Through a daily give and take between father and son, at times fought in the trenches, we are discovering an overriding bond. The bad days remain but it seems now there are more good ones.

Even in the most difficult times, my earliest vision of having two boys has survived. And Miguel has never lost excitement about the prospects of a younger sibling, even when I waivered. He desperately wants a full-time playmate to once again call brother. Although he only sees Javier from time to time, the two clearly share a strong connection. I curb his enthusiasm, knowing the journey to adopt a second child is a complicated and emotional process. Making my way to the finish line with a second child is not a done deal and will be difficult, but this is consistent with all that I have learned about parenthood: good things come from hard work.

"I want that one! I want that one!" Miguel screams pointing out the car window at a random boy walking with his mother along the sidewalk. This has become a regular occurrence. Just last week, at the start of communion, he leaned over, pointed from the pews, and shouted for all to hear, "That one Dad, that one." He easily confuses our trips to the mall pet store with the burdensome process of adoption. It's understandable when viewed through his eyes.

My journey to Antigua, Guatemala, has come several years after my initial entry into the state adoption system. Although Miguel and I had a tumultuous start, social workers have given me high marks. Through the challenging transition, I've learned a lot and can apply a long list of parenting lessons to a second child. To my surprise, I was unable to crack the code a second time and successfully adopt another child from the state system. Before I reached this conclusion, I rode a tragic emotional roller coaster.

As with my first adoption, I sought placement of a Hispanic boy between the ages of two and four. Miguel, five years old and now a kindergartner, would once again be able to be the older brother. Social workers supported this direction and thought Miguel would do well with a younger sibling. With thousands of available children awaiting adoption in the State of Arizona, how could I not feel better about my odds this time around? Several friends encouraged me to consider adopting internationally to avoid the bias against gay parents within the state system. But I remained committed to working within Arizona and the child welfare program, not to mention the thirty thousand dollars I didn't have to work with a private adoption agency.

"Think global. Act local." Every day I passed these bumper stickers and each time they reenergized my commitment. I was convinced these were a divine message, assuring me a child was somewhere within the state. My profile was solid: upstanding citizen, a close extended family, a live-in nanny, secure job, and a sibling at home. However, one thing had not changed; I was a gay man. It took little time to begin to run into familiar road blocks. With Cyndi, my former social worker, long gone from the system, I had no advocate to defend or recommend me for a placement. On paper, plain and simple, I remained a liability. After more than a year in the system, it was again clear that until every last married couple had been assigned a healthy child, I wouldn't be selected.

Roberto was my wake-up call and the catalyst for my search abroad. My aunt, a long-time Head Start teacher, called me with the boy's story. He was a new student placed in her class and living with a foster family while he awaited adoption. Roberto's family had abandoned him several times and yet legally Child Protective Services was required to look for any extended family members who might be willing to take him. Through their search, social workers discovered family members living in Globe, a small mining town sixty miles east of Phoenix. Roberto left my aunt's class only to return two months later after his extended family decided they didn't want him after all. The boy moved back into the same foster family and this time around was officially cleared for adoption.

"Roberto's back! And, I talked with his foster mother," my aunt explained, excited and out of breath. "I have the name of his social worker. He's going to be adopted this time and you need to call quickly if you want to be considered." Anxiously, I asked, "Is he a good kid?" Her response was immediate. "Oh yeah, he's a great kid with so much potential. He just needs a break," my aunt reassured me. Later that day, she shared photos of Roberto with me. He was three years old, two years younger than Miguel. His face was happy, his smile sweet and genuine. His dark black hair was wet and sweaty, but he looked healthy. Like Miguel, all reports indicated Roberto needed stability and someone who would love him and not send him away. Once and for all, he needed someone to take full responsibility. And yet, after all he'd been through, he appeared content and resilient. Even through all of the disruption, he was thriving. A child's resilience remains one of the great mysteries of life and one of God's greatest gifts.

The next morning I called Roberto's case worker, who was friendly but not optimistic that I would be selected. She indicated that although no one surfaced and expressed an interest in Roberto, he'd likely be assigned to a two parent family. "He has special needs," she reminded me, indicating that she had yet to read my adoption file. "Wouldn't you want someone who understands this little boy and knows what he is going through?" I asked. I reminded her that I already adopted one boy with special needs and I had a live-in Spanish speaking babysitter. She appeared unimpressed. I began to spout my resume: good job, education, large extended family, practicing Catholic and bilingual. She remained passive and detached.

A week later, sensing things were not going well, I called the caseworker's supervisor. She was friendly but sounded like she was reading from the same script as her subordinate. She repeated that I was an unlikely selection for Roberto. "He has special needs and we have determined that he'd do better with a two parent family," she parroted. "Which two parent family?" I asked, desperately. "All the while you look for this magical two parent family, this boy rots in the system!" After a year, I'd grown angry and defensive and as a result it would soon turn awkward. "I want this boy…I want this boy NOW! Name me one other person on this earth that wants this boy as much as I do." I began to cry. "Tell me the name of any family in the state of Arizona that wants this boy more than me. I want their name!" I grew embarrassed by my display of emotion and worked to quickly end the call. The truth was now before me. Once and for all, I had shut the door for good. "I'm sorry," I said. "It's just that I've been in this system for a year, fully approved and awaiting placement, and now you are sending me to a foreign country to adopt a child—So much for acting locally."

• • •

"*Nosotros no mordemos.*" We don't bite, I assure Ana again, trying to entice her to join us at the kitchen table at the end of a very long day. She laughs as she picks up her plate with pizza and salad; she grabs her can of Diet Coke and sits at the table. Miguel is all smiles as she plops down next to him.

Carmen was right. Ana will be a good match. I am relieved. A young grandmother, in her late forties, Ana is full of energy. Quiet in our initial conversations, she and Miguel carry on animated conversations throughout the day. She's attractive but timid, wounded in some way. I know little more than she's in the process of a divorce and has a daughter whom I've met, who is well-mannered. Her grown son lives with his father back in their hometown of Hermosillo, Mexico, an eight hour drive from Phoenix. Although she's reserved, I sense there's a vitality that has been pushed back into the recesses of her soul. Ever-guarded, she has a youthful side which surfaces from time to time as we go about the grueling task of moving into our new home. She's quick to catch herself when these girl-like spells surface, quickly directing them back to the periphery. She seems conflicted but appears comfortable and at ease with us.

After dinner, I insist Ana call it quits. She's resolute that more boxes can be unpacked before the night is over. "*Siempre, hay mañana,*" I tell her. "There is always tomorrow," I repeat in English, forever second-guessing my Spanish. She relents and sits on pillows with me and Miguel; we watch *Chitty Chitty Bang Bang*. Miguel and I have begun watching Disney classics from our neighborhood library. Cable won't be activated until later in the week, so we're grateful for the video, which distracts us from our weariness. "*Yo ví esta película con mis hijos cuando eran niños.*" Ana says it's been years since she's watched this movie with her own children. Her guard lowered, she laughs often throughout the film.

After our busy day, bedtime comes early. Once Miguel changes into his pajamas and brushes his teeth, Ana asks if she can put him to bed. I kiss him goodnight and listen outside the door as she reads a Spanish translation of *Curious George*. Miguel is much like the little monkey—barely able to contain his curiosity. Inevitably, George's enthusiasm leads him to trouble. However, his guardian, the single man with the yellow hat, can't find it within himself to scold Curious George for his unique gift of wonder. My son's own curiosity leaves him exhausted from our big move. Tonight he has only enough energy to gently close his eyes and sleep. Ana sets the book on the unpacked box serving as a nightstand, and kisses him on the forehead.

"*El es un ángel,*" Ana whispers as she steps from his room. She looks upward and asks God to bless our new house and my son. Her gratitude is humbling. I'm overwhelmed in the moment by her unselfish spirit. She heads to her room but turns before entering. "*Juan, gracias por su hospitalidad,*" she says. I assure her it is Miguel and I who are blessed to have her as part of our family.

Over the next several weeks, I take Miguel door-to-door as we introduce ourselves as the "new kids on the block." Several of our neighbors seem surprised to see us at their doorstep. I'm shocked at just how many of them don't know one another. Ana joins us for a number of these informal meet-and-greets, no doubt generating speculation with each stop. Within days of our arrival, I've flushed out a good number of boys who are Miguel's age. I happily volunteer our front yard as a neighborhood play zone. Sitting in Adirondack chairs on the front porch, Ana and I enjoy watching the boisterous pack of five and six year-old boys gather on our lawn to play baseball and tag.

Over the course of several weeks I learn more about Ana. We drink ice tea and talk, directing our attention to the boys whenever we're unsure how to fill the silence. Our conversation never feels uncomfortable or forced. I respect Ana's strength and integrity. Although I know little of her path, she's courageous and dignified. She's like a wounded vet, who is filled with honor regarding her service. Her children are her source of pride. Guarded about her past, she frequently talks of what a nice life we have and how she enjoys living with us. In so many words, she speaks of this period as her refuge. She feels torn being with us but is clearly happy. She says that life is difficult without her husband and son, but better than if she were back in Mexico. She is vague about whether she is separated or working toward a divorce. I sense this part of her story is yet to be written.

One Friday afternoon, while sitting on the porch, Ana is recruited by Miguel to play baseball with him and the neighborhood boys. Miguel directs Ana to the pitcher's mound, where she appears, by size alone, to be the captain of this rag tag team. Her four pint-sized teammates are spread around the makeshift baseball field that is our front yard. Miguel stands at first base; I recognize my red baseball glove, which lies in the grass and serves as the base. He looks intently at the opposing team; there are four boys who wait impatiently to bat. A skinny athletic boy from around the block stands at home plate, cutting the whiffle ball bat back and forth. He's very focused on his swing. Ana lobs the plastic whiffle ball over home plate. The batter nails it, sending it high over the other boys' heads and into the neighbor's front yard, where it lodges into a large cholla cactus. Miguel and his teammates rush to the ball and attempt to remove it from the sharp plant. Ana quickly grabs a mop that is drying in the sun, and uses the handle to pluck the ball from danger. The boy has long since crossed home plate and shouts, "I'm falling asleep here waiting for you guys."

Later, it's Ana's turn. Though she appears uncertain how to stand or hold the yellow plastic bat, she remains undeterred. The boys laugh as she swings and misses the ball over and over again. The pitcher eventually relents, lobbing the ball underhand. She laughs at herself when she connects with the ball, barely a dribble beyond her feet. Miguel pushes Ana forward yelling, "Run, run!" She outruns the pitcher and makes it safely to first. She pumps her fist in the air, while jumping up and down in excitement. For the first time since her arrival, she's uncensored and alive, and filled with joy. Her worry and despair are briefly banished, pushed south of the border. As she crosses home plate, she high-fives each of her teammates. Her miniature playmates happily chant, "Ana,

Ana, Ana..." Seeing Miguel carefree and in the mix, high-fiving his friends and nanny, is tangible evidence of progress.

With each changing of the guard, it takes several weeks for the schedule to reset and feel routine. Ana walks Miguel to school each morning, returning to pick him up at 2:10 p.m. The chain link fence is lined with stay-at-home moms waiting for their children as they come running through the open gate. Another group of mothers in SUVs and minivans forms a long line and is directed one-by-one through a maze of red cones. Frequently confused as Miguel's mother, Ana stands quietly among the moms. She is unable to respond in English to these women's queries. and learns to smile graciously as they unintentionally talk around her, most unaware that she doesn't understand English.

"*Puedes ayudarme con el Inglés?*" Ana asks eagerly one night at the dinner table if I'll help her learn English. She explains that she wants to communicate with the other mothers at the school gate and better understand Miguel and his friends. Later that night, I pull out my college Spanish books. Instinctively, I begin to place Post-it Notes with the appropriate English words on much of the furniture and appliances throughout the house. Miguel helps me pin the notes onto various clothing, towels, sheets, and blankets. Paulina's legacy lives on. By the end of the night, our house looks like a thrift store on the verge of a closeout sale.

Miguel takes Ana by the hand as we repeat the English and Spanish word for each item. Ana repeats the English words quietly, seemingly embarrassed by her translation. Quickly, Miguel runs to his room and returns with a small plastic megaphone. "*El cuadro*" Miguel yells through the little red megaphone as we pass a picture hanging on the wall. He stops and waits for Ana's English translation. "*La puerta*" he continues as we walk through the bathroom doorway. Ana and I laugh as we go from room to room.

At the end of the night, I find Miguel in his pajamas, snuggled up to Ana in her bed and watching a Spanish soap opera. He's enthralled by all the drama. He refuses to go to sleep unless Ana, and only Ana, puts him to bed. She swoops Miguel up like an airplane.

She's carefree and animated as she prepares to land him in front of the bathroom sink. I imagine her as a young mother with her own children, overflowing with youthful energy, vitality, and love. She understands that Miguel and I both love and want her here. She's blossomed from the affections of a five year old boy and his father. Ana senses our need for her presence and has flourished knowing she has a meaningful role and is a necessary part of our family. The reticent and shy woman that first graced our doorstep is slowly transforming herself. As Miguel brushes his teeth, she sings and is once again happy.

This night is a turning point and from here on, Ana is seemingly unburdened. For the time being, years of neglect and abuse are locked away. With each passing day she evolves and reconnects with herself. Early Saturday morning, I awake to witness both Ana and Miguel crawling on their hands and knees through my bedroom. I detect their movement from the reflection of the mirror in the bathroom. I remain still. Miguel is signaling to her to crawl on her belly to get lower and avoid detection. Half asleep, I have no idea what the goal is. Miguel appears to be in the middle of a military tactic, as Ana, his dutiful recruit, crawls closely behind. Slowly, both pull the covers from my bed, Miguel targeting the bedspread while Ana quickly grabs the blanket. I am left with a single sheet. The two giggle as they swiftly crawl from my room and not so quietly shut the door. Not yet 7:00 a.m., I go back to sleep. An hour later, I rise to find a virtual kingdom of blankets and tunnels running throughout the house. Dining room chairs, patio furniture, and tables are connected through a series of blankets and sheets. Somewhere, lost among the maze of linens and things, are my son and his nanny.

"*Hola.*" I hear a peep from the other end of the tunnel, which appears to terminate in the guest bedroom. Now I am crawling, delicately, making my way through the tunnel. "*Hola, Hola,*" I hear Ana's voice confirming her participation in this farce. As I turn a corner, I must squirm on my belly as I pass through the narrow tunnel in the hallway to avoid pulling down the entire structure. I make my way to the spare bedroom, which has a series of stuffed animals standing guard.

"General Waldron, your captain seeks permission to enter," I call out the request before entering the bedroom. "It's okay Dad, you can come in," Miguel says as he clears the animals from my path. The two have built a taller gathering area in the guest bedroom. Both Ana and Miguel sit cross-legged, eating cereal, and laughing at me as I try to pull myself up without knocking over the entire fort. My son has waited for my arrival. A bowl of cereal serves as my reward for successfully completing the winding journey. He pours milk from a jug he's hijacked from the refrigerator. "Pretty neat… huh Dad?" he asks.

Our life with Ana is good. Whether it is our new house or the forward movement of our lives, I struggle less and less with Paulina's departure. The continual comparisons have slowly faded. Our refrigerator is now plastered with Miguel's art projects. His new interest in all that is wood has left our garage littered with half-completed woodworking projects. Miguel seems to understand that Ana brings a different set of skills to the table than Paulina. Ana can't help him complete his birdhouse, but she's there for him when he strikes his finger hard with the hammer. Ana is a mother and instinctively knows what to do. Miguel senses this and often chooses to run to her first for his comfort when he needs it. She provides a tender love, which fills a void left absent from his tumultuous beginnings. In these times, he allows himself to be cuddled and cared for; he resists the temptation to push away the intimacy of a loving touch or caress. It's an odd twist of fate that the children who miss out on early parental love spend the rest of their lives pushing affection and intimacy away. To see Miguel allow this love to infiltrate his hardened shell is overwhelming.

Miguel still has defined battlegrounds. The most difficult terrain remains bedtime. Most nights he continues to defy sleep. His only wish is to hang on to the present. He wants nothing to do with saying goodbye to daylight or welcoming the darkness. His mental to-do list is always long and as a result he's impatient for the new day. At all costs, this is worth a battle. He channels his energy into deconstructing anything orderly in his room. When he's in this mode, his toys are thrown about and his bed torn apart. Any of my attempts to quiet him are futile. However, Ana is welcome. Never at first, but after an angry rebuff or two, the door slowly opens, serving as a signal to enter. Like Paulina, she has a way of talking with him that brings relief from the rage and uncontrollable surge of anger that still consumes him. I'm not fully privy to what happens behind these doors, but the result is always the same. Sometimes it's minutes, other times it's an hour, but in the end Ana steps from the room of a slumbering child. Whatever she is doing nourishes and calms him, allowing him to finally turn off the noise and confusion of his past.

For several weeks and for no apparent reason, Ana begins to distance herself from us. After dinner, she is no longer interested in taking walks and she discourages Miguel from coming into her room and snuggling up next to her when it's bedtime. She cries after she talks with her son living in Mexico. Some of her confidence appears to be eroding, and with it her smile seems to have lost its way. And then Ana announces she must return to Mexico to finalize her divorce. After just five months, this is unexpected. Because of our seamless routine, the news comes harder this time around and I feel like I've been sucker-punched.

Ana asks me to consider holding her job for six months as she gets her life back on track. She's genuine in her request and tells me how much her time here has changed her for the better. "*No, no puedo*" I say, despondent but realistic that I cannot hold her position. I have a six year-old and a pending adoption, which makes this impossible. Very soon, I'll have two boys who will need more than my two hands to shepherd them. I am decidedly unenthusiastic about having to search once again for another nanny, but search I must. Ana can give me no assurance that she will return, so I hold the line and reconfirm that I can't wait. As I shut off the lights in the kitchen and prepare the house for bedtime, I hear Ana weeping softly. I'm sad for all of us.

Ana is quiet and withdrawn as her daughter places her bags in the car. Her confidence and energy have evaporated. She sits in the passenger side of the vehicle refusing eye contact, desperately avoiding a tearful goodbye. Just as they pull away, Miguel comes barreling through the backyard gate. Clutching a sunflower, he runs alongside the accelerating car, shouting, "*Te amo! Te amo!*" Ana directs her daughter to stop, rolls down the window, and takes the sunflower and kisses him. "*Te voy a extrañar,*" she says through tears. She will miss him. It's all too much for her. Then she begins to sob as the car moves forward. For the first time, Miguel cries as another nanny drives away.

FOURTEEN

No, no, no…I'm not a Priest!

We're across from one another; Rosa directs her grown daughter, Carolina, to sit to my left as she balances a small cream-colored, weathered photo album on her lap. It's been several months since Ana's departure and I'm once again on the hunt. For nearly two months I have procrastinated, putting off a new search because it's become harder and harder to trust. It's not so much that I don't believe the women I interview, but now I better understand the impossible situations they face. Over the years, the candidates I've met have been earnest in their desire to care for my son, each assuring me quite convincingly that their primary interest was to create a new life in the United States. But pulled between two worlds and separated from their families, they were left with few options but to float illegally between two lands. As it should be, their ultimate loyalty is to their own families, not mine.

Opening her family album, Rosa begins to speak in Spanish. Proudly, she shows me pictures of her home in Hermosillo, Mexico, as I tell her our last nanny, Ana, was from there as well. I'm surprised by the size and significance of her home, which looks very much like one of the many Southwestern style houses located on our street. This is where she raised her three children, all now grown. Carolina, her youngest, who sits attentively next to her mother, has recently returned after graduating from college and is working for a Mexican telecommunications company. Alejandra, the eldest, is married and lives close to her parents with her husband, Jesus, and her three year-old daughter, Daniela. Mauricio, her middle child and only son, and his wife, Gabriela, recently had their first child, Francisco. Carolina tells me about her boyfriend, who studies law and hopes to be an attorney one day. She mentions she and her siblings have all attended college, each spending at least one semester at an American school. Rosa shares proudly that all her children are fluent in English.

Turning the pages, Rosa points to a man dressed in a brown leisure suit; the photo's caption reads "1981," the year I graduated from high school. Mother and daughter laugh. "He looks so macho," says Carolina in English. Armando, the man with three children in tow, is Rosa's husband. He's a road contractor and business owner in Mexico, where he builds streets and other infrastructure. As she fingers through the album, I see pictures of Rosa as a young woman and photos with Armando on their wedding day. Rosa is beautiful and vibrant in these pictures; her husband appears stiff in his suit but he projects pride. A large extended family surrounds them.

Photos of children follow. There is Carolina posing in a puffy red dress with black patent leather shoes, and Alejandra sitting atop the handlebars of her brother's bike. They look carefree and unburdened. Rosa fills with pride as she points to a photo of her granddaughter, Daniela. "*Ella es mi preciosa,*" she says. "*No hay cosa más importante que los niños.*" She has the same sanctity for children that I've seen from the many Mexican women I've interviewed before her, though she has a more contemporary and modern sensibility than the others.

Rosa is attractive and looks younger than her age. I estimate she's in her late forties, possibly her early fifties. Her hair looks newly styled, she's wearing perfume, and she's dressed with a great deal of thought for our meeting, with her clothes neatly pressed. Carolina looks like a model. She's beautiful and curvaceous, and wearing designer jeans with a white summer blouse and gold sandals. Her long brown hair is set off with highlights. Friendly and outgoing, she effortlessly interchanges between Spanish and English to help facilitate the discussion, which feels natural and relaxed.

Taking a more serious turn, Carolina indicates they will return to Mexico tomorrow morning. "Times are bad, really bad in our country," Carolina explains for her mother. "My dad's work is not going well—our government is very corrupt." She explains that her father's business has all but evaporated due to a recent election and a specific elected official who has blacklisted her father's business because he refused to support his campaign. I learn that Rosa must work in the United States to help support her family. She explains that she has several friends, like herself, that live in the United States, having left family behind for the same reason.

This is not Rosa's first time seeking employment here. She shows me a photo of two young children. For a short time, Rosa worked for a single mom. Recently divorced, the woman needed help and found Rosa through the classified ads. Carolina gives me the woman's name and number, as well as a list of other handwritten references.

The final photo in the book is a family portrait of Armando and Rosa surrounded by their grown children, in-laws, and grandchildren. Her family is beautiful; she looks proud and complete. Rosa's presence is powerful, and though she's eager to work, she's a calm and confident woman. It seems her life experience and struggles have made her resilient, but no less compassionate.

"*Usted es un sacerdote?*" Rosa asks me as she looks over my shoulder. I'm confused by the question until I realize she's referring to crosses of all shapes and sizes that hang on the wall near my dining room table. "No, no, no…I'm not a priest!" I say first in Spanish and then again in English. *Far from it*, I think to myself. Rosa remains transfixed by the many crosses so I focus my energy on Carolina. "Please, please tell your mom that they were gifts." A few years back, I made the mistake of buying several crosses at a flea market and now every birthday and Christmas the collection grows. Once my message is understood, we laugh.

I'm taken by Rosa, her daughter, and their family living some 350 miles away. Their photos look so much like the ones that line my parents' hallway and fill our numerous family albums. From bell-bottoms to polyester, they capture similar childhood memories and milestones of baptisms, children's birthday parties, youth sporting events, graduations, and weddings. Special occasions that are the foundation of a family and worthy of memorializing for future generations, these images validate a life lived well. Though small in physical size, Rosa's photo album speaks volumes about who she is and what she values. More importantly, it explains why she sits before me. Regardless of where we call home, family photos help reinforce what we hold sacred in our lives.

"Juan, above all else love your family," Rosa says with help from her daughter. She holds eye contact to re-enforce her message. Plain and simple, her dreams are inextricably tied to those of her children. Her journey to this country is much more about providing opportunity for them than resurrecting her own ambitions. This is what motivates her to move from all that she's known. Soon I will better understand the full significance of our meeting and how it will serve as a catalyst for her entire family and their fulfillment of the American dream.

Charging through the front door, Miguel returns from a friend's house, and interrupts Rosa in mid-sentence. Instinctively, her arms extend as she continues talking. My son is magnetically drawn to her. Rosa squeezes his cheeks and kisses him on both sides of his face. "*Mi precioso*," she says over and over. Surprisingly, Miguel is relaxed and stays locked within her embrace. She removes the hair from his eyes and is enamored by his dimples.

"*Tu eres muy guapo y tienes buenos modales.*" She compliments Miguel, telling him what a handsome and well-mannered boy he is. I thank her and express how blessed I am to have him in my life. She addresses Miguel, and asks his age and which sports he likes to play. Having raised three children, this is familiar territory. She's in her element and speaks with complete ease. When he becomes quiet and shy, she knows just what to do; she lifts him up and places him on her lap and shows him her photos. Miguel is instantly curious and engaged as he asks questions about the many new faces that unfold before him. "That one is my granddaughter," confirms Rosa.

We talk about the future. I tell Rosa that I will soon be adopting a second child from Guatemala. If all goes well, Oscar will join our family. "Is she up for the demands of two small boys?" I have Carolina ask her mom in Spanish to ensure nothing is lost in my rusty translation. I'm concerned that two energetic boys may be more than she can handle at her age. "She wants lots of grandchildren," Carolina interprets her mother's response. "This will be good practice."

I review the living arrangements in greater detail. With three nannies having come and gone in less than two years, I feel like our home has a revolving front door. Rosa is excited about having her own room off from the kitchen. She explains that on weekends she can either stay with us or live with relatives, whatever works best. Her extended family has lived in Phoenix for many years.

Miguel is now talkative and eager to show Rosa his room and the bedroom we've prepared for Oscar. He pulls her hand as he leads her from room to room. "Do you like Mexican food?" Carolina asks as we tour the kitchen. "My mom's a great cook."

"Are you here legally?" I ask the two women as we again sit on the couch in the living room. It's now time for a reality check. "Do you have valid visas?" I can no longer avoid this issue. Paulina, Carmen, and Ana have left me no other choice but to ask. I need to protect my son from further disruption. With each departure there's been a break in continuity and a resulting struggle to reconnect. With the changing of the guard, there is a required dance of sorts to create a meeting of the minds, a necessary re-sync of discipline and ground rules. With the many early upheavals and changes in Miguel's short life, it's not easy for him to recalibrate, not to mention for me. Ultimately, Miguel, and soon Oscar, will need stability to prosper.

Carolina pulls out two passports which I examine closely. They look authentic. "We have travel visas and are free to pass from Mexico to the U.S. Don't worry, we're legal," she laughs nervously. They appear genuine in their conviction. Carolina explains they must renew their passports every six months, but that they're welcome visitors in this country. With so many Mexicans forced to travel illegally across the border, I'm compelled to ask how they were granted travel visas. "My dad has his business and owns property in Mexico, so we have never had a problem with visas," Carolina clarifies. With relatives and friends living in Phoenix and Tucson, Rosa and her family have spent their entire lives traveling freely across the border. They seem to know this city better than some locals do.

"How will you handle being separated from your family?" I ask Rosa, concerned that I will hire her only to see her make the same heart-wrenching decision to return to her family as Ana did. She explains her children are grown and that she has few options for work but to live apart from them. They don't need her in the same way that they did when they were Miguel's age. Her husband will visit on the occasional weekend and stay with relatives. "It will work, don't worry," Carolina says with a smile. But given our recent track record, how can I not? Just before they depart, Carolina mentions Rosa has two other interviews for nanny positions later in the day.

As soon we say our goodbyes, I call the single mom who employed Rosa. "She's amazing. She was such a huge help at a difficult time in my life." She goes on to describe a loving and playful woman; a hard worker with a caring heart. She recommends Rosa without reservation. I call two others on the reference list and leave messages. Within the hour, I reach Carolina on her cell phone and let her know that Rosa has the job. She will return from Mexico in one week to begin work.

Over the next week, I prepare for Rosa's arrival. I head to the grocery store to stock up on food and cleaning supplies; I wander up and down the aisles, unsure of which choices to make. "My mother loves to cook," Carolina reminded me in our last phone conversation. To make matters worse, invariably I shop when I'm hungry. Resentful, I eye the many mothers with their detailed shopping lists, working each aisle systematically as a coach might work a playbook. I notice some of them organize their lists based on where items fall within the store. In awe, I pick up their discarded shopping lists and gaze at them as if they were mysterious and sacred scripture.

One mother in particular catches my attention. She's large and in charge. She holds a fistful of coupons in one hand, and clutches a leash with a toddler attached to it in the other. Although the leash appears a bit extreme, her command of the aisles is impressive. She pushes an overflowing cart, strategically passing certain aisles as she barks out orders to her two older children. Dutifully, they respond, disappearing for short periods of time only to return waving the items in the air as if in victory. The children are well trained. Perhaps they've graduated from a boot camp for peewee shopping fanatics. More impressive, they don't return with candy or chocolate-covered cereal and attempt to hide it among the many other items, like I did when I was young. Nor do they whine about their feet hurting or fight with one another. This mother is a precise surgeon, and her children the attending nurses.

Later at checkout, we stand at adjacent registers. Her execution is flawless to the end and her coupons have saved her more than eighty dollars. I on the other hand, have no game plan and no coupons, along with no rhyme or reason to what I buy. As a result, I default to a predictable list of standbys: spaghetti and pasta sauce, hamburger patties and buns, packages of chicken breasts, beans and tortillas, hot dogs, eggs, milk, cheese, pickles, packaged lettuce, Frosted Flakes and oatmeal. Mr. Clean and Lysol are just two of the many cleaning products I include. Thrown in for good measure are a fifteen dollar mop and ten dollar broom, to replace the ragged ones at home. Finally added to the conveyer belt are several packages of sponges and yellow plastic gloves.

Rosa arrives on Saturday morning with one large suitcase and her own bucket full of cleaning supplies. Miguel is at a friend's house for the night and won't see her until the morning. She's shocked at what she discovers under the kitchen sink, and within minutes playfully scolds me for purchasing cleaning products at the grocery store. She tells me that I need to start shopping at the dollar store for better deals and laughs as she opens the freezer and sees seven packages of chicken breasts, hamburger patties, and multiple bags of French fries. "*Le gusta el pollo?*" It's true that I do like chicken, but the reality is that I'm not a particularly good or adventuresome cook. Rosa's arrival promises to jumpstart our tired routine and finally provide more variety in our diet. She makes it clear that dinner is a spiritual time. We'll grow stronger and closer by all eating together. She needs no invitation to make herself comfortable in the kitchen.

Rosa holds up the new fancy mop I purchased at the grocery store, which is still covered in plastic. She again playfully shakes her finger at me, insisting I've overpaid and that I must return it and buy one at the dollar store. The same goes for the broom and dustpan. I cringe as she holds up a tin can that serves as my spice rack. Bottles of garlic powder and cinnamon sit alone in the huge container. Once she surveys the many empty kitchen shelves, she hands me a lengthy list of groceries to purchase.

Almost immediately, the smell of Lysol returns. Like clockwork, dinner is underway each night when I return from work. Rosa does wonders with the many packages of frozen chicken breasts and soon I start referring to her as "*La Maga,*" the magician. In turn, Miguel takes the sheet from his bed and ties it around Rosa's neck to create a cape. He gives her a stick and a top hat. She wears her magician outfit with pride as she prepares dinner.

Before going to sleep, Miguel snuggles next to Rosa on her bed. With each nanny has come a unique bedtime routine. That first week, she tells him stories of her family back in Mexico, of her children when they were small. He yearns for more details and asks question after question. One story is of her son, Mauricio, when he was a little boy, pitching for his neighborhood team in a game that came down to one strike. His father, Armando, was his coach and walked out to the obviously nervous Mauricio in an effort to relieve the building tension. Armando secretly whispered into his son's ear and then left the pitcher's mound. The boy calmed himself, took a big breath, and fired a final strike to win the game.

"What did he tell him? What did he tell him?" Miguel asks Rosa. She whispers something into his ear and he lights up with a large smile. Whatever it is, it strikes a chord with my young son. This time around there is something more personal and permanent, a bond that seems more complete. I cannot put my finger on it other than to explain that it just feels right.

Two months later, Alejandra and her daughter, Daniela, come for a visit. I insist they stay with us and leave work early to greet them. As I enter the house, Rosa is nowhere to be found. Alejandra dances to Shakira, jumping around the room, her arms swaying freely from side to side. With the volume cranked high, Daniela follows suit. I remain unnoticed as they giggle and laugh, intentionally bumping one another.

Alejandra screams as I walk up from behind and tap her shoulder and introduce myself. She is flushed red and clearly embarrassed as she quickly turns the music down. Unaware of my presence, Daniela innocently continues to sing out, her back still turned. She screeches as she faces me. We both laugh at the little girl's reaction.

I'm happy the two are here. The separation from family has been hard on Rosa. Her loneliness comes as no surprise, for they are the single reason she's here. I've learned so much from my nannies, the most important lesson being that when they are happy, I am happy. Alejandra's arrival is sure to bring Rosa endless joy.

Rosa and Miguel return from a neighbor's house. Alejandra and I laugh as we tell Rosa about the spontaneous dance party. The women quickly work out the sleeping arrangements: Alejandra will sleep with her mother on the full bed in Rosa's room, and though the small bedroom, now piled high with suitcases, has no room for Daniela to sleep, Rosa insists she join them. Over the objections of both women, I place Daniela in the extra bedroom that will soon be Oscar's. Miguel will be close by and this will allow him the opportunity to practice for his new role as big brother.

Alejandra and I sit at the kitchen table as we get further acquainted and talk about what the future holds. Like her sister, Alejandra is beautiful. She's slimmer than Carolina, and has the confidence of her mother. Rosa is in the front yard and watches Miguel and Daniela play with a group of neighborhood children. Screams and giggles leak through an otherwise quiet house. Alejandra has something on her mind and now tells me she is moving to the United States with her daughter. Once she's settled, her husband, Jesus, will follow. She wants to find an apartment close by so that she can be near her mother. It's clear that her visit is less of a vacation and more of a scouting trip. The suitcases stacked in the bedroom do not contain Rosa's possessions, but rather Alejandra and Daniela's belongings. Alejandra speaks of a fresh start and of new opportunities. "Mexico is very depressing," she says from across the kitchen table. "There's no reason for me or my family to stay."

She wants to find a job that will allow her to support her family. Fluent in English, Alejandra is sure she can do it. She's ambitious and positive about what the future holds, but her tone changes as she discusses her husband. She's less confident about his willingness to relocate and his prospects here. He doesn't share her enthusiasm about moving to a new country. Speaking only Spanish, he will likely be limited to factory work, or more difficult yet, day laboring. Although she shares none of the details, I sense the two have had many heated discussions. Both will leave large families and many friends behind. Technically, she's not permitted to work within the United States, and yet she'll disregard immigration laws, like millions of others, to better the life of her child and her family. As Alejandra talks of her difficult decision to relocate, I'm struck by the magnitude of separation for so many throughout Mexico and Central America. How many mothers and fathers have made this same journey across the border and left loved ones behind? Yet, given the chance between opportunity and a future without hope, no law will ever suppress a willing human spirit.

Through the large windows in the front of the house, we see a group of children playing with Rosa. Each grabbing a hand, Miguel and Daniela pull Rosa through the sprinklers, as the rest of the small army pushes her from behind. Again and again, they run through the water, as their faces reflect the cool relief from the hot summer. Alejandra and I see her mother trip over the sprinkler and fall to the ground. We both run to the front door, but by the time we reach her, Miguel, Daniela, and a handful of neighborhood kids are on top of her. They begin chanting, "Dog pile, dog pile, dog pile..." Rosa makes her way out from under the mound of small children on top of her, covered in grass and soaked from head to toe. She laughs uncontrollably as she hugs the children. "Alejandra, you can stay as long as you like," I say as I look directly into her eyes. "You and your family are always welcome."

Within two weeks of her arrival, Alejandra has signed a lease for an apartment within walking distance of my house. The complex, one of the largest in Phoenix, feels like a resort. The sprawling development has four swimming pools, each anchored by a Jacuzzi. Meandering streams run through the grounds, creating several lakes. Most patios open to the sound of running water and long stretches of turf create the feeling of an oasis within the desert. Alejandra tells Rosa and me about the many amenities: sand volleyball, a movie theater, tennis and basketball courts, bar, dry cleaner, and a convenience store.

Alejandra has negotiated an amazing deal on her new place, which has recently changed ownership. Apparently, one of the stipulations for financing is a requirement by the new owners to allocate a sizeable number of units for low-income renters. Working with the Spanish-speaking rental agent, Alejandra was able to qualify for the new discounted rate. She'll pay less than $500 a month for a one-bedroom apartment; a good deal by any standard, and far below the market rate.

I'm impressed with Alejandra's ability to forge her way. She has no intention of looking back and will immediately return to Mexico to gather additional belongings. In less than one month, she'll begin her new life. Although her future is uncertain, she's determined to make it better. "I'm scared, but I just know things will work out," Alejandra says, just before driving away. Daniela is perched high in the seat, happy and looking out the back window as we wave goodbye.

FIFTEEN

Blame Game

A group of neighbors has gathered across the street from my front yard. Idling, I await the opening of the garage door. They nervously wave and huddle closer, making like a cyclone. They're animated and unusually suspicious. I don't know what has happened, but on this night I sense a disruption in our household's routine.

Rosa has made the transition an easy one, and we are in the zone. Each night I race home from work to ensure we eat dinner on time. I've committed to leave the office no later than 5:15 p.m. so this can happen. Most nights, dinner is nearly ready as I enter through the garage door, the kitchen bathed in a tasty aroma. Tonight it is barbeque chicken topped with corn salsa. Rosa has taken to placing a shopping list on the refrigerator door in an effort to encourage me to buy something other than chicken. This week's list includes *Carne* at the top with *TAMALES* in all capital letters. "I could eat tamales every night," Miguel says after he asks me to read the list to him.

"*Rosa, que pasó con los vecinos?*" I ask my nanny why our neighbors have gathered across the street. She leans back from the kitchen sink to look through the large living room window, unaware of the impromptu crowd. Collectively they crane and swoop their necks to look in at us as if we're animals in a zoo. Uncertain, Rosa and I look at one another. "*No, sé.*" She tells me she doesn't know. That makes two of us.

"Hey there," I say to my neighbors as I open the front door. "How's everyone doing tonight?" The group appears hesitant to answer. Upon our arrival less than a year ago, each of them went out of their way to be kind. Many lived here for years, long since raising their children, with several now enjoying their roles as grandparents. Our front yard has the informal designation as the neighborhood play zone; the increased activity encourages them to gather around our houses and more freely mingle. "Can we talk to you for a minute?" ask my neighbors, Carol and Jim, a couple in their fifties, who've lived in the same house for more than twenty years. They're kind and genuine in their interest to be good neighbors, even leaving a stocking for Miguel on the front door Christmas morning. They guide me away from the restless group. "We have some concerns about your nanny," they say in a soothing yet accusatory tone. I'm at a complete loss as to what is unfolding before me when Carol asks, "How well do you know Rosa and her family?" I remain quiet as the interrogation unfolds, but a growing agitation begins to simmer. "We think she's the one breaking into the houses," she states casually, unfazed by her accusation. From a distance, I see neighbors looking our way.

There has been a rash of break-ins over the last two months. Consequently, I remind Rosa and Miguel to lock the front door before leaving each morning for school. Like clockwork, the two exit at 7:30 a.m. and walk the three blocks north to the neighborhood elementary school; Rosa returns home to do chores until it's time to collect Miguel. Surely this restless crowd doesn't suspect Rosa is a thief breaking into neighborhood homes? *Tell me this isn't happening.*

Disoriented, I look beyond the small crowd and see Rosa through the living room window; she's setting the dining room table. Carol and Jim talk of their suspicions but I stop listening. Again, Rosa passes the large picture window. She now hugs Miguel in her arms; they're laughing. "John, John…John," Carol repeats herself several times to pull me back into the conversation. "There are people who come and go while you are at work. There is this young Mexican guy who keeps dropping things off. Yesterday he had a couch and T.V. He doesn't stay long and then he is off." Her fears have gotten the best of her and she becomes shrill. "Is it possible that Rosa is using your house to stash stolen goods?" No longer is Rosa the sole perpetrator; I am now an accomplice.

Do they really believe I am hosting a stash house? How have we gone from loving nanny to drug cartel madam? Just last week, Rosa called me at work to tell me she was unable to unlock the front door when she returned from walking Miguel to school. She asked Jim and Carol to use their phone. When I returned home that day, I confirmed with Carol and Jim that the lock on my front door indeed needed to be changed and that they might want to keep a close eye out as one of them is usually home most days. "This is happening a lot in your neighborhood," the locksmith reported once he had completed the work. "Make sure to lock those doors," he said. "You don't want any harm coming to your nanny and your little guy."

Rosa is no more a crook than Betty Crocker; her children, no more thieves than the Mousketeers. What Carol and Jim don't know is that Mauricio, Rosa's son, is in the process of moving his young family to Phoenix. He's moved furniture on the weekends from Hermosillo and is storing it, along with boxes, in our garage. I'm disappointed in my neighbors; there are no two ways around it. I want to make a run for it, dash into the house, and grab Rosa's photo album. I want to sit with each and every one of these unlikely vigilantes and show them pictures of Rosa and her family, much the same way Rosa and Carolina first sat with me. Somehow these images might make them understand she is an extension of all of us and not some common criminal. As Jim and Carol awkwardly maneuver through the final pieces of this misconceived discussion, the other neighbors continue to crane and twist their necks while looking in at Miguel and Rosa.

"Look, I can assure you Rosa is no more a suspect in these break-ins than yourselves. She has not moved three hundred miles from her home to pillage and steal; she's here to work…end of story!" And as for the young Mexican man who has come and gone, I clarify to the crowd that this is Rosa's son, who is in the process of moving his wife and young child to Phoenix. Far from a criminal, Mauricio is eternally polite, a hard worker, and industrious, cut from his mother's cloak.

"I think we're done here," I say abruptly to Carol and Jim. "Let's stay focused on criminals, not nannies." I am unable to prevent this final barb as I turn and walk away. I cross the street to face the group of persistent and nosy neighbors who remain stationary near my front door. "Time to disperse people, the sideshow is over." I walk in between them to clear out the crowd. I allow the door to slam behind me to send a clear signal that I am pissed off.

"*Un momento,*" I say curtly to Rosa upon entering the house. I cannot dull the sound of defiance in my voice. I'm wounded but remain focused. Rosa and Miguel are poised at the dinner table. He is hungry, while she looks concerned. "Dad, it's time to eat!" My anxious son yells out, as I turn and walk quickly down the hallway. "We need to say grace," Miguel yells out. "One minute Bud, I'll be right there," I shout back, attempting to gain my composure. Quietly, I enter Miguel's bedroom on the other end of the house and gently shut the door. I'm pressed against a wall and hidden from the view of the still gathered neighbors. I peer out the long narrow window, careful not to be seen. The group has now converged around Carol and Jim, peppering them with questions. I'm breathing hard and in a state of shock. I look around Miguel's room. Thanks to Rosa, it remains orderly. Miguel's stuffed animal, Andy the Armadillo, peaks out from the comforter. Transfixed, I stare at my neighbors. I've yet to see this group unite or organize around anything as they have tonight. I am incredulous; their evidence is shameful. Rosa is a foreigner and speaks little English. She's not one of them. Most important, she's Mexican. It is apparent, no other evidence is necessary.

Mauricio has rented a two-bedroom apartment in Villa Privada, a newer complex on the edge of North Mountain Park. The series of two-story buildings hug the desert mountain preserve and the compact grounds feature several pools and spas that are just five minutes from my house. Mauricio chose the apartment to be close to his mother and his sister. As her only son, Mauricio holds a special place in Rosa's heart. Mauricio's wife, Gabriela, and son, Francisco, will move north in several weeks. Like his sister and mother, he carries a travel visa. Over the years, he's crossed back and forth through the border. His English is good and he has a mind for business. A fan of motivational speakers Tony Robbins and Zig Ziglar, he's upbeat about his future and potential opportunities. Mauricio's optimism is contagious.

In no time, he finds a job selling MoneyGram services in a Mexican meat market in an effort to compete with the many corner check-cashing stores that serve the burgeoning number of Hispanic immigrants who are unable to secure a traditional bank account. The World Bank estimates more than twenty billion dollars each year is wired to Mexico from immigrants living in the United States. This flow of money has become a lifeline for many families that remain in both large and small cities south of the border. In Phoenix, these check-cashing stores are now as common as the corner McDonald's. Several of the busiest of these new enterprises are former fast food restaurants that went belly up. A former Long John Silver's restaurant is now called *Fast Cash,* featuring a children's play area and blinking neon signs to lure undocumented workers who have few other banking options. A former Taco Bell is now *Easy Cash* and just down the street a Church's Chicken and adjacent Payless Shoe Store have been converted as well. For those who make so little, it's ironic that there are so many vying for their money. Mauricio is quick to point out that this job is not his end game, but rather a place to start and where he hopes to rekindle his dreams. He's excited about the opportunities that exist in this country, and I can't help but share his enthusiasm.

"I want to start my own business," he says. "I'm not sure what kind, but something." He sees the many Hispanic people living around him and senses prosperity. He wants to help them in some meaningful way with their transitions by offering a useful product or service to make their journeys easier and more successful. In his short life, he's traveled many paths. He attended a community college in Tucson, went to trade school for air conditioning repair, and has worked as an auto mechanic, but none of these tapped his true calling as a businessman. His short term goal is to get a valid work permit to open many more doors. His hope is that an employer will sponsor him and that this will lead to legal work. Until then, he embraces his new sales role.

Just down the road from her brother, Alejandra is now fully settled with her husband and daughter. Several days a week, Rosa watches Daniela as Alejandra looks for work. Daniela is now four years old and spends mornings in preschool at a nearby church. Miguel, now a first grader, still enjoys playing with her when he returns from school, and loves the attention of his new extended family. As well, our home has become the central gathering spot for Rosa and her family.

Early one Sunday, Alejandra and Jesus stop by my house after checking out our neighborhood's annual garage sale. The event is a big deal and attracts Phoenix residents from throughout the city, who hope to find deals. Alejandra and Jesus have purchased two bikes and ask if they can store them at our house until they can bring over their vehicle to pick them up. Alejandra is thrilled with their purchase. Both bikes are clearly weathered and likely twenty years old, but look to be in good working condition. They remind me of an orange ten speed that my parents bought me for Christmas from JC Penney years ago.

Immediately, it's clear the couple has been fighting. Alejandra is upset but smiles as she speaks in English. "He doesn't like the bikes…he doesn't like anything right now," she says. Jesus is agitated. "*No te gustan las bicicletas?*" I ask Jesus if he dislikes his new purchases. "*No, me gustan,*" he answers without a smile. There is tension between the two of them that has nothing to do with the bikes positioned between them. "I like them…they're retro." I say to Alejandra trying to lighten the tension. "You can have mine and I will take yours," Jesus responds in Spanish, as he abruptly turns and departs.

Jesus, who works in a produce factory, has struggled since his arrival. Unable to speak English and without a work permit, he's clearly frustrated. "I'm sorry, John. Jesus is very unhappy and wants to move back to Hermosillo," Alejandra confesses. "*Lo siento.*" I tell her that I'm sorry. "Oh, by the way, John, I got a job." Her mood changes for the better. "I am going to be teaching Spanish to… how do you say it? To bosses? *Executivos?*" She struggles to explain. "Executives?" I attempt to clarify. "Yeah, yeah that's it…executives." She's very excited about her prospects and will be classified as an independent contractor, not an employee. This will allow her to work under the radar of growing immigration reform. Within two weeks, Jesus will return to Mexico with no intention of rejoining his wife and child. Soon after, they'll file for divorce.

• • •

An afternoon appointment cancels and rather than return to the office, I head home. "Surprise," I say loudly as I walk through the garage door. The house is cool and quiet with the exception of the muffled sounds of laughter and talking coming from the backyard. I hear splashing and music.

Through the windows, I see Rosa, her family, and my son. I stand in the kitchen and cherish the moment. The sheer volume of activity brings me happiness as I remain invisible to the crowd gathered outside. The music is loud; there is giggling, and the children play tag with Mauricio between two sets of pool stairs. Francisco holds his father's neck tightly as Mauricio swims awkwardly to ensure his young son's head remains above the water. Miguel and Daniela squeal as Mauricio growls like a bear and lunges for them, just missing as they reach the steps safely. Francisco laughs at his father.

Carolina, Alejandra, and Rosa huddle on green plastic lawn chairs around the table in what little shade remains from the sun high overhead. Gabriela, Mauricio's wife, sits close-by on the pool deck, cooling her feet in the water. I recognize her from her pictures. Everyone wears a swimsuit except Rosa, who is terrified of water. She's dressed in shorts, a red blouse, and fashionable sandals. Even in the scorching sun, she looks elegant and beautiful. The women laugh at Mauricio and the children swimming in the pool. A pitcher of iced tea, chips and salsa, and a large bowl of grapes sit on the table. Kids' clothes and beach towels litter the pool deck. Overflowing from horseplay, most of the towels are sopping wet.

I have work to complete and calls to make, yet I opt to change into my swimsuit. "Cannonball!" I yell as I open the French doors leading from the family room directly to the swimming pool. All three children scream out in surprise as I create a large splash. Unintentionally, I soak Gabriela.

The women laugh as I surface. "*Lo siento, lo siento, lo siento,*" I apologize several times to Gabriela. This is our first meeting and we're both embarrassed. "*Mucho gusto.*" I attempt to rebound by introducing myself. Mauricio and his sisters laugh hysterically. "*Igualmente.*" Gabriela can't stop laughing either, as she mops the water from her face. She's petite and beautiful, even when drenched. The kids begin splashing, directing their energy on the women sitting around the table. The women quickly retreat into the house as children's screams fill the air. Mayhem erupts and I am flooded with happiness.

Weeks later, police cars swarm the neighborhood. Patrol vehicles scurry up and down the adjacent streets as a helicopter hovers overhead. Low to the ground, one block over, it remains stationary. The blades rotate quickly, creating a steady, loud, angry noise. My neighbors gather. I wave but they're distracted by the whipping sound above. "What's going on?" I yell out. "No one knows," Jim responds loudly, his eyes affixed above. "Police have been swarming the neighborhood for several hours." "I hope they catch the bad guys," I scream out over the commotion. This is the first time we've talked since he and his wife held their sidewalk interrogation several weeks before.

Later that night, I brush my teeth at the start of the ten o'clock news. The hum of my electric toothbrush drowns out the news anchor's tease of the lead story. But the location of the live shot is familiar; it's my neighbor's house. I recognize the wood shingles and the odd yard art on the retro 1960s home. The reporter stands in the front yard. Familiar neighbors are gathered around her. I make my way to the set of our large living room windows and see the sky aglow and the green cable dish hoisted high from the news van. I sit inches from the television on the edge of my bed. An overly enthusiastic blond reporter indicates that police have apprehended a robbery suspect in my neighborhood. The suspect was caught burglarizing the home positioned behind the reporter. When arrested, he had a variety of tools in his pocket that were used to gain entry. They believe he is likely the same individual involved in a spree of other robberies in the neighborhood. The young man was arrested along with two other men of interest. Videotape of the suspect, a Caucasian male in his early twenties, flashes quickly across the screen. Speculation of drug use is mentioned.

Early the next morning, I back the car out of the garage. I see my neighbor, Carol, in the rearview mirror; she approaches quickly. She knocks and her face fills the driver's side window. "I'm so sorry," she says as I roll my window down. Her face looks pained and sad. She grabs my arm gently as it rests on the steering wheel. "I'm sorry about what we said about Rosa and her family. Please forgive us." She turns quickly and retreats to her house. I roll the window up and drive away. Redemption feels bittersweet.

SIXTEEN

No Turning Back

Dr. Jack Carpenter and I meet at his office in a nondescript executive suite, just off the Black Canyon Freeway, which snakes throughout Phoenix. As part of a second adoption process, I'm required to have another psychological assessment conducted by a mental health professional. Now in the final stages of an international adoption, this meeting is an important remaining step. The results will be sent to the Northern California agency, which has been critical in helping me navigate through a complex Guatemalan adoption. They have a successful track record of placing children with gay parents, and months back helped to identify Oscar, a three year-old boy who lives in an orphanage in Antigua. It's one of a few in the country that is open to working with gay men and has indicated that my adoption, if all goes well, could happen within months.

Although I've been analyzed and scrutinized many times throughout Miguel's adoption, the process isn't any more comfortable the second time around. The doctor shares the space with an accountant, a salesman, and an insurance broker. A single secretary assists each of them and directs me to sit in the small waiting area. Dr. Jack, as he likes to be called, is tall and lanky; he wears oversized glasses and looks more like a nerdy engineer than a thoughtful shrink. I'm nervous as I hand him the two-sided paper that must be completed. He's just one of many "professionals" who have the ability to prevent me from fatherhood a second time around.

I know little about Dr. Jack, other than he was recommended by a mother in my single parent adoption group who has assured me he's kind and open-minded. "I see that you're a single parent. Why do you want to be a father again?" he asks immediately, after some perfunctory small talk. "I've always wanted to make a difference," I tell him. "It's easy as a single man, especially a gay man, to get lost in yourself. I've always felt like I had a calling to be a father and adopt two boys." Growing up Catholic, I tell Dr. Jack, I thought I would get married someday, even though I knew I was different from a very early age. "The church discourages you from acknowledging your sexuality as a child and as a result I became really good at denying my attraction toward men." It would take many years for me to successfully connect faith and my sexuality. The road getting there was a bumpy one.

I disclose to Dr. Jack that I was in therapy in my early twenties with a Catholic psychologist who would later become a major figure head within the change therapy movement. The therapist was writing his first book, charging a reduced fee, and encouraging me to attend both individual and group sessions with other men like myself. At the time I was clueless about the emerging and contentious nature of conversion therapy and was just relieved to find other men who struggled with their sexual identity. For a while, the sessions seemingly helped resolve a nagging disconnect between male identity, sexuality, and faith. I enjoyed sports and working out, and at some basic level had a sexual attraction toward women. As a result, I became one of the therapist's star pupils.

Dr. Jack's note-taking is at a near frenetic pace with each passing disclosure. Intentionally, I gloss over several relationships with men within the therapy group before focusing on two longer term relationships with women that followed. "At the core of change therapy is repairing a broken male image and identity." As I attempt to justify this therapeutic approach, it sounds foolish and I feel duped. Relationships with women were treated as "homework" and an integral part of the intervention. Embarrassed, I look for a way out of the conversation and this misguided time of my life.

"I'm still coming to appreciate we're all born in the likeness of God," I respond conclusively, moving the conversation to the here and now. Wanting to leave this painful time behind, I attempt to neatly wrap things up. "In a nutshell, I wouldn't allow myself to love another man," I tell him sounding more definitive. "I would feel guilty and find ways to end these relationships quickly. These days, I live a different reality. It's that plain and simple." I see clearly on Dr. Jack's face that he doesn't believe any of this is plain or simple, but I remain hesitant to delve further into the past.

With good reason I worry about disclosing weakness and frailties to Dr. Jack, especially regarding my sexuality and the resulting journey of acceptance. Many have encouraged me to embrace a "Don't Ask, Don't Tell" policy as I work to adopt a second son. As I learned with Miguel, the State of Arizona Child Protective Services works to place children first with two parent heterosexual couples, while disallowing gay partnered couples to adopt altogether. This leaves older, more challenged children for single gay candidates. Although there are exceptions to these policies, they are rare. This is how I've come to narrow my search for a second child to Guatemala; they are one of the few countries that permit a single man to adopt. Although I've been ambiguous in my responses on official paperwork in the past, today I choose to share the truth.

"When were you able to finally admit that you were gay?" Dr. Jack asks. "My break-up with Jane was the final straw," I tell him. "Was it difficult?" He follows up. "Yeah, but after that, there was no turning back." I exhale deeply while reclining in my chair. Tentatively, I begin to recount the tipping point.

I met Jane in a young adult Catholic singles group at a church in West L.A. Relationships like Jane came easy. Single Catholic women in their late twenties yearned to be wives and mothers and were excited to find a man who talked of wanting children; even better, I wanted two. Sexual intimacy with Jane filled a pressing need and allowed me to suppress my inability to fully commit emotionally to her. Although I enjoyed the physical contact, I was left feeling lonely and disconnected. I stayed with her longer than I should have because I held onto the dream of children and a traditional family. Jane and I shared faith, which encouraged me to push aside the fundamental reality of my sexuality. And furthermore, I had embraced a therapeutic intervention that validated dishonesty.

When we finally broke up after nearly a year, there was guilt. Jane had spent months investing in me in hopes that I was the answer to motherhood and her dreams of wedded bliss. From our first meeting, Jane was ready for marriage. After dating for six months, she began a full court press. She talked often about her need for a life-long commitment. "We're so comfortable together," she often said. And, she was right; at some level, we were an easy and comfortable pair, and as result our time together stretched much longer than my feelings for her.

In the end, I was no different from the other men who had wronged her. Jane's previous boyfriend was a recreational drug user and compulsive cheater. I was now in his company. I had a different set of reasons, but for Jane the outcome remained the same. She was again in the unenviable position to search for not only a boyfriend but a husband and father, in Los Angeles of all places. I was added to a long list of undesirables, whom she had miscast as "husband."

With the break-up, I was again at a crossroads. My prayers grew increasingly confrontational, angry, and frantic. "Will I ever find someone to love? Will I ever become a father? Who am I meant to be?" During these times, my mind raced and I found it near impossible to be silent and listen. I prayed earnestly, "God, bring me clarity." I sought comfort and peace through a higher power, yet was unwilling to be quiet and still—likely terrified of the impending response.

I explain to Dr. Jack that at those times, the only way to calm my fear and anxiety was to place an imaginary grey wool blanket over my many thoughts and distractions. It came down to this very basic visual exercise. Each night, I would kneel by my bedside in hopes of finding the truth. Only when I shut down my long list of wants and needs did the message finally present itself. In my most vulnerable moments, I surrendered to the image of the heavy blanket resting over my worries and in these quiet moments of reflection, I felt relief from his presence. Most importantly, I finally heard his message.

"What's the message you heard?" Dr. Jack asks. "The truth will set you free." Again, I repeat it, "The truth will set you free." No doubt, delayed from a lifetime of denial and years in conversion therapy, a path of acceptance and truth was finally possible. I tell Dr. Jack that thereafter I embraced the divinity of truth that was set before me and I was finally enlightened. With that, the doctor closed his notebook and our session came to an end.

SEVENTEEN

A Guatemalan Gift

As the large wooden gates roll open, children from all directions come running. A giggling gaggle of them gathers around me and my brother, Kevin. With their beautiful brown complexions, black hair, and radiant smiles, they're a sight to behold. They jump up and down in excitement, desperate to see what's concealed in several plastic shopping bags we're carrying.

We're not alone among the many children, who are safe behind bulky non-descript white adobe walls that serve as a barrier from the overwhelming hardship of this country. Anyone driving down this alley would mistake this site for any one of the many residences in this modest but charming historic town. A small group of prospective parents from around the world has come to this residential neighborhood in Antigua, Guatemala, an hour's journey from the severe poverty of the country's capital, Guatemala City, in hopes of meeting a future son or daughter.

My brother is at my side to support me in this unique yet informal interview process. We stand in the front yard compound of the toddler house, one of two dwellings for orphans who've been abandoned by their impoverished parents. An active volcano sits just outside this quiet neighborhood and is unmistakable from all angles. Smoke wafts from the cavernous spout and is ominous as the children play, oblivious to the natural wonder just beyond. On the porch, toys are strewn everywhere. Children happily poke and prod at little drums and play telephones. "Which one is Oscar?" I struggle to hear my brother ask above the contented noise.

Kevin and I hold either end of a jump rope while girls take turns running through the swirling chord. There is a brief scuffle between boys who fight with one another to secure one of the three available swings. All the while, a group of attentive women outfitted in light blue nurse-like uniforms watches lovingly over the children to ensure they're safe; they whisper and smile at the parading group of prospective parents. They're kind and humble, and appear fiercely proud of the outcome of their labor. There's no mistaking their success as rambunctious little bodies dart in and around them, stopping regularly for hugs and praise. The children call for help as they struggle to perch themselves atop the large green slide or ask to be pushed higher on the swing set. Others want to be consoled after falling down and scraping a knee. A quick affectionate touch and everything is better. All knowing, these women have the power to turn tears into laughter. Their presence brings relief and comfort.

My decision to adopt a second son from Guatemala has been all-consuming. The outcome of this trip is irrefutable; one that will last forever. This time around, I'm in an unfamiliar setting, which has increased my anxiety. When all is said and done, the adoption will cost me more than thirty thousand dollars. I've taken a loan out on my 401K, which cleaned out what little I had to show for retirement to date.

My time here is short; less than four days. Joseph, the American born orphanage director, has matched me with Oscar. Once we meet, the choice will be mine, but I have to be quick. So far, I've seen photos and read a brief description. What if he's not the one? After all that I've been through with Miguel, do I even know what it really means to be "the one?" However, as I look at the flock of happy children, I'm certain this place feels right.

The women who care for these children create a sense of equilibrium and seem to be the critical link—the secret of success, the foundation for all happiness that percolates throughout the compound. They appear to share a set of values with Rosa, as well as the other nannies that have come into my life. Somewhat like Joseph, I have relied on female caregivers to help steady the course and be a consistent and loving presence day in and day out.

Rosa is my safety net and Miguel's guardian while I'm away. Earlier in the morning, I phoned home and talked with him. Bursting with excitement, he was playing in the backyard with Rosa's grandchildren, Daniela and Francisco. Later, the two older ones will go swimming and then with Rosa's family, they'll enjoy a barbeque. After it cools, the children will draw chalk figures of Oscar on the driveway. Always watchful and ever-present, Rosa's removes any worries about home.

A group of ten or so vocal boys trails my brother and me as they eagerly await the moment we reveal the contents of the plastic bags, which we carry high over their heads to ensure a surprise. I was told to bring small toys and games that would help engage the children in play. It's clear they want for little. They're loved, and as a result jubilant and carefree except for one little boy who's been crying nearly non-stop. After Joseph provides us with a quick tour of the grounds, my brother and I sit with the children, who instinctively form a circle. Several boys have climbed the shade tree above to gain an aerial view. Overhead, they giggle back and forth as they strain their necks to see inside the bags. From the organized manner in which the kids have gathered, it's obvious that many have come before us to this tranquil place to claim one to call their own.

I pull out several small containers of finger puppets; Kevin and I pass them out among the group of excited children, as tigers, elephants, pigs, porcupines, and cows begin to come to life. Ensuring we've not forgotten about them, we throw several up to the boys who are perched among the tree branches above, yelling, "*Aqui, aqui.*" It becomes instantly clear that this is a new experience for all of them as we make our way through the crowd, showing them how to squeeze their small fingers into the puppets while making animal noises. More children come running to the ever widening circle—all are eager to participate. I create an impromptu chorus by instructing the children to yell out "Moooo." Next up, the elephants.

The children laugh and chase each other through the walled playground. There is a chaos of happiness that builds from within. Animal sounds are coming from all directions—children are giggling and having fun. From this insulated spot, the poverty of this country is invisible. Gone are the guerillas and abductions fueled by civil unrest. Behind these gates, all is peaceful and good.

With all the activity, I've forgotten about Oscar, my primary reason for this long journey. A loud whistle rings out as the children dutifully gather in a line of smiling faces in front of Joseph. "Papa, Papa" they sing out prior to asking what seems like a million questions. Surrounded by the ring of attentive caretakers, Joseph serves as a surrogate father for this loving brood. He knows each of the children by name and all have at least one nickname. Now, entirely focused on identifying Oscar, I ask my brother if he knows which one he is.

When Joseph is done, all the children are present and accounted for, with the exception of the one little boy who continues screaming and is unwilling to move from his corner perch. The ever-persistent caretaker works diligently to coax him from the pipes of the water fountain. He screams out in terror as she finally pulls him free. She quickly hugs him tightly to soften his fear. She and the little boy join the others who remain in a single file line. The women quickly gather around the screaming boy. They whisper softly, intermittently rubbing his back in an effort to calm him.

"Oscar, everything will be okay. It's all good little man. No more tears," Joseph says to the little boy as he wipes away his tears. My heart sinks as I realize that this is the boy that I have traveled more than 2,500 miles to meet. Among the many happy and giggling children, there is just one that is hysterical and terrified: Oscar.

Through several e-mails, Joseph has indicated that Oscar is available for adoption and feels like he'd be a good match for me and Miguel. As I see the terrified boy before me, I'm at a loss for words. I'm so deep into my own terror that I refuse to move toward the child. *Why this kid?* I repeat over and over again in my mind. There's a yard full of giddy children and yet I am stuck with the crying boy. *Why?*

I refuse to move or go over to the hysterical boy, hoping there's been some mistake. I deny any recognition of callousness. Joseph directs Clara, one of the blue-clad caretakers, to bring Oscar to me. Once the boy understands a handoff is underway, he cries harder. There must be a mistake. Maybe Joseph misunderstood and is unaware just how full my plate is with my son. Although we've come a long way, we still have such a difficult journey ahead. I was meticulous and clear in my e-mails to Joseph. He must know that I need an emotionally stable child. My instincts tell me that this isn't a good match. Above all else, I want and need happy. *Give me one of the happy ones*, my inner voice screams.

Clara looks away quickly as she hands Oscar off to me. "He just needs to warm up to you," Joseph says, walking up to me. With the screaming, he must repeat himself to be heard over the boy's cries. Within seconds, Oscar is hyperventilating and desperate for breath. He's depleted what seems like gallons of tears as he stiffens his arms to maximize his distance from me. He's galvanized with terror. I glance at the other parents, who look relieved not to be in my shoes. Ever the trooper, my brother pulls out all the stops in an effort to make Oscar smile. He has a zebra puppet on his finger as he tries to distract Oscar from his mounting terror. The boy only screams louder. Kevin is unfazed. He grabs a bright red rubber ball from his pocket and begins bouncing it up and down, "Look Oscar, look," he says calmly. Over and over he bounces the ball but Oscar won't stop. My anxiety grows. I am shutting down.

"No worries, he just needs to get to know you," Joseph says again as he dismisses the kids and staff and takes Oscar from my arms. Later in the afternoon, Oscar will come to our hotel for a visit. Joseph is convinced some one-on-one time will calm the child and turn the tide of terror. Once the screaming boy has been removed from my arms, I remain traumatized. I've been through so much with Miguel, but despite his rage and fury, I have yet to experience this level of fear. Even at his angriest, Miguel doesn't desire to be anywhere else but with me. Oscar, however, wants nothing to do with me. As I look at the tropical sanctuary that is his home, and at the loving women who care for the children, I can't blame him. It's peaceful and safe here. This is all that he knows. He smells it. Change is in the air. He's a fighter, resistant to the bitter end.

• • •

The taxi circles the corner and stops abruptly in front of the old rustic hotel. The rickety cab has no seatbelts and as a result, passengers must brace themselves to avoid hitting the windshield. Clara is in the front seat with Oscar, still trying to comfort him. "*Vamos a regressar en tres horas.*" The nanny informs me that she'll return in three hours to reclaim him. In an instant she's gone, and I'm left on the corner with the screaming boy. More than ever, I'm aware of pedestrians looking at us. Inches from us are a Guatemalan mother, barefoot, in a dirty colorful native dress, and her three young children; they're sitting at the curb. A blanket full of native dolls and flutes lay on display for the occasional exiting tourist from the nearby hotels. She looks depleted and weary, but manages a smile that reveals her brown teeth as she points to her blanket of wares. "*No gracias,*" I respond loudly over Oscar's screams. I carry the boy back to our room which faces out to a small grassy courtyard. Oscar is delirious with fear. His cries echo through the empty hallway and up through the courtyard and out onto the street. My brother has a worried look on his face as he opens the door. I can't imagine being here without him. A father of two boys, he's calmed and cured many a crying fit in his day. "Hey Oscar, I have a football for you," Kevin says while handing him the ball." I repeat the phrase in Spanish, "*Oscar, esta pelota es para ti.*" Oscar throws the small yellow plastic ball back at Kevin.

Oscar is again hyperventilating. He inhales shallow pockets of air between the deafening wails as we sit on one of two rocking chairs. "Shhhh," I say to the boy. "Shhhh…" I have nothing else to offer. I'm in shock and not thinking clearly. Despondent, I want nothing more than to calm this little boy. I mirror the actions of the many caretakers I witnessed earlier in the day. I rub his back gently as I sing *Rock-a-by Baby* quietly into his ear. Hoping for distraction, Kevin suggests playing with Oscar in the grassy courtyard. My brother grabs the small football, a Frisbee, and the big bouncy yellow ball that we purchased at the open air market. I attempt to set Oscar free on the grass but for someone so intent upon rejecting me, he won't relinquish his grip.

With his arms locked so tightly around my neck, I struggle to breathe. I pry him free as heads peer in and out quickly from several doors of the hotel rooms that encircle the grassy area. What must these guests think of the two white men and the hysterics coming from the terrified brown skinned boy? I worry that someone may call the police. Yesterday, as we made our way through the *Parque Central*, the town center, my brother and I saw two guards riding on a Pepsi truck, both toting machine guns. They stationed themselves at the door of the small convenience store as the driver wheeled in cases of soda. This image fresh on my mind, I suspect we may be at some risk in this third world country, appearing to hold a small boy against his will. I convince my brother to return to our hotel room.

When Oscar leaves, and I've deemed the visit a disaster, I decide to pray at the ancient Catholic church one short block from our hotel. Antigua is filled with the ruins of colonial churches and historic buildings that once anchored this former capital. "Lord, what do I do?" I'm exhausted and confused and seek guidance. I have just one day remaining to decide whether or not to go ahead with Oscar's adoption. My search has gone on more than two years and I've invested thousands of dollars through the process. "Lord, you say you bestow upon us only that which we can handle…I can't handle this." Sitting in the stiff pew, I drift in an out of sleep as a constant stream of people pass. A crowd kneels in front of a statue of the Virgin Mary; she looks sad and gravely concerned. Dozing in and out doesn't help me escape feelings of sadness and agony. After a time, I look at the suffering image of Jesus on the cross and hear a gentle cadence. A familiar phrase repeats over and over in my head. "The truth will set you free."

"I can't adopt Oscar," I blurt out to my brother, out of breadth after sprinting back to the hotel room. I say it over and over upon entering, afraid that if I wait a second longer I may change my mind. "I just don't think he's the one." Later that night I call Joseph and tell him the same thing. "I just don't think Oscar is a good fit for my family. I think he needs a two parent family." I get the irony of these words as they leave my mouth. "Are there any other children that we met today that are available for adoption?" I ask earnestly. "Eduaro, Pedro, and Enrique," Joseph says curtly. "Come back tomorrow at 9:00 a.m. and I will introduce you to them."

The children run wildly toward us as the wooden gates are once again rolled open. Immediately, they tug at our sides and pull at our hands in their effort to draw us into play. The same group of boys is following my brother and me as we push them on the swings and help them up the slides. Again, the women stand guard throughout the yard. Clara is in the corner with Oscar, who actively shields himself from me. My heart aches as we lock eyes one final time and he screams in fear.

With less than two hours to spend with this marauding group of children, I fixate on the familiar smiling boys who gather at our sides. I replace my feeling of guilt with a practical search and rescue mentality. I focus on finding three boys: Eduardo, Pedro, and Enrique. "*Como te llamas?*" I ask each one. Indeed, two of the boys are present within our small group. Eduardo is the most outspoken and handsome of the bunch. He's five and athletic, and throws a football back and forth to my brother. Polite and smaller than the younger boys who gather around him, he's likeable and happy. Pedro is shy and hangs close to Eduardo, taking turns catching the football. Tall and lanky for his age, he has brown front teeth and, I sense, a genuine and loving soul.

As I sit under a grassy tree with several of the boys, asking them basic questions about what they had for breakfast or which is their favorite toy, I detect there's one small and funny boy with brown bangs and chubby cheeks. He continually jumps on my back and each time I pull him over into my lap. This sends him into laughing fits of hysterics. He's one of the boys from yesterday who was high up in the tree, smiling and eager to see the contents of the plastic shopping bags. "*Como te llamas?*" I ask the little boy who is upside down in my lap. He's wearing green polyester shorts and a white and green striped cotton t-shirt. "Pepito," he says. I am busy searching for Enrique, the final boy who I am unable to identify, yet this little boy with the adorable smile, who continues to be glued to me is slowly capturing my attention. I begin to play hot potato with Eduardo, Pedro, and several other children. As we pass the ball around, faster and faster, Pepito continues to jump on my back and enjoys the falling motion each time landing safely in my lap. His persistence is impressive. "Don't forget me," his continual pratfalls seem to be saying.

He plays easily with Eduardo and Pedro. They sing out each other's names as they pass the football. Joseph has not mentioned a "Pepito" as one of the children available for adoption. I survey the grounds several times as my brother and I engage the children in an effort to find the elusive Enrique. First, I must find Joseph and clarify where Enrique is in "the process." I've learned over the last six months that it may take more than two years before a child is free for adoption. There are many hurdles that must first be cleared through the Guatemalan court system. After lingering in the Arizona State Adoption system and with Miguel now six, I must narrow my choice to only the children that Joseph indicates will soon be available. With less than thirty minutes remaining before our taxi is to arrive, Joseph appears through the wooden gates. He's come to formally introduce me to the three available boys and appears in no hurry. I've been told there are other parents coming in the next day or two who will also be selecting children. I must make my choice before I leave.

"Where is Enrique?" I ask Joseph desperately as he approaches. "He's hanging on your back," he says, slightly annoyed that I've rebuffed his original match with Oscar. "The boy says his name is Pepito, not Enrique," I respond quickly. "Pepito is his nickname; we have three other Enriques, so we have nicknames for each of them." I let the boy with the persistent and infectious smile fall one final time into my lap; I turn and face him and then we embrace for what seems like a lifetime.

• • •

"Welcome home," the yard sign reads. My new son runs quickly past and through the front door. A sense of arrival crosses his chubby cheeks as he grabs his older brother's hand, now his tour guide. Miguel is gentle and sweet and talks in a quiet and soothing tone. "Welcome home Enrique." He bends over and hugs his brother tightly. On the long journey home, we switched back to calling Enrique by his given name, which seems to make him happy. Miguel has been a patient big brother, waiting for this day. It's taken more than six months since that first meeting to work our way through the Guatemalan courts, which throughout has been touch and go about approving international adoptions. There's growing concern among Guatemalan leaders that far too many of their children are being adopted outside the country and there is real talk of shutting down international adoptions altogether. With my two boys standing before me, hand-in-hand, I feel especially grateful.

Rosa cannot refrain from kissing Enrique repeatedly on the cheeks. After months of nothing more than photos and videos sent to us from Joseph and his staff, we now all vie for his attention. Before any tour of the house can begin, his grandparents must also have their turn. Enrique no longer has to share his living space or caregivers with dozens of other orphans; it's now just his new family, in what must appear to be a mansion to this little boy. Will he miss Clara, his favorite caretaker? What about his many small amigos? Several months from now, will he even remember Joseph, the orphanage director and surrogate father?

In great detail, Miguel guides his miniature sibling through each room of our home. "*Aquí…aquí*," Enrique points to the doorway as he pulls his big brother to the next room. My mom and dad, Rosa, and several family members trail closely behind; we're all visibly overcome with emotion at the sight of the two brothers almost connected as one. It's hard not to smile as they attempt to communicate back and forth. Miguel makes every effort to speak in Spanish and demonstrate his vocabulary. "Enrique, your room is *grande, sí?*" Miguel asks as we reach Enrique's bedroom. "You have a big *cama* to sleep in."

Enrique is visibly excited about his new surroundings and walks on the tip of his toes, unable to ground his feet from all his enthusiasm. From the toy box in the corner of Enrique's room, Miguel plucks out a soccer ball and placing it under one arm, uses the other to pick up his little brother. He heads to the grassy front yard, as Enrique laughs easily, while dangling from his brother's side. As they kick the soccer ball back and forth, Enrique misses and falls to the ground. Concerned, Miguel runs over and picks him up like a baby. Neighbors gather and Miguel carries him to them like a large sack of potatoes, showing off our newest arrival. Rosa and I smile at one another as neighbors encircle the two boys. All at once, they begin asking Enrique questions and through it all he remains smiling.

Working through separation anxiety, Enrique spends the next four nights crying himself to sleep. I stand over the bed, rubbing his back, singing "Hush little baby." When I stop, he begins a faint melodic cry. Within an hour, he falls asleep. After the fourth night, the crying ends. Like clockwork, he's able to recalculate and fully accept his new world. From here on out, at the drop of the hat, he falls asleep in his car seat and wholeheartedly allows himself to collapse against me as I carry him to bed. Intrinsically, he trusts. Enrique is not compelled to fight authority or push away love. He appears comfortable and happy within his own skin. He blends easily with his pack of new school buddies, and in no time they're inseparable. He learns English quickly and soon resists speaking

Spanish with Rosa. Can the transition be this seamless? Is this really it?

From the beginning, Enrique has no interest in looking back or anchoring himself to the past. "Pick me, pick me," he practically shouted during our first encounter at the orphanage. Over and over, falling into my lap, he was certain I would catch him and then keep him. At some basic level, he knew a better life waited beyond the big wooden gates. He kissed each of his Guatemalan caregivers goodbye, many crying as they passed him down the line. As we walked from the orphanage onto the cobblestoned streets, he proudly positioned himself upon my shoulders. From there, I sensed he could see the large smoldering volcano and the promising future that lay beyond.

I can only surmise that the successful transition underway has less to do with what I'm doing and much more to do with those who loved him from the start. The unconditional love and bond between child and caregiver will forever serve as an endowment in life, creating a sense of well-being within, allowing one to weather many difficult journeys. Much can be done to counteract a disruptive beginning, but nothing can replace the sense of contentedness that comes from the earliest bonds of affection.

EIGHTEEN

The Golden Rule

"There must be something in the water down there," one of the mothers whispers as she leans over to get my attention. "All of them are so happy." A group of tittering children jumps on a large trampoline, while several of the youngest swing on a play set positioned on the opposite end of the backyard. For the last thirty minutes, Enrique and Miguel have bounced up and down, with no end in sight. They're sweaty and their brown skin glistens in the bright sun on this Sunday afternoon.

"Are those your two?" the same woman asks, looking in the direction of my boys. "Was your wife not able to attend?" I clarify I'm a single parent with no wife in the picture and two adopted sons. Unfazed, she points to her son who is currently teaching a group of children how to do a flip, while jumping high in the air. Enrique is fearless as he attempts a summersault and lands on his brother, who cushions the blow. Both are quickly up and jumping again, no worse for the wear. The woman's son is Miguel's age and like most of the children gathered in the backyard, was adopted from Guatemala. I'm part of an informal support group for parents who have adopted Guatemalan children and this is one of several gatherings that will occur over the next year.

"I don't know how you do it as a single parent," she says kindly. "You know you are violating a fundamental rule of parenting:

Don't let the kids outnumber the parents." We laugh and then I tell her how fortunate I am to have such a supportive extended family, always willing to help. I mention Rosa and the other nannies that have come before her and how they've been such an important part of our lives. She's interested to learn more about the nannies, how I found them, and where they come from. Given the growing negative sentiment in Arizona regarding illegal immigrants, I play it safe and keep my response vague. She jokes that she would trade my nanny for her husband any day of the week to help her handle the many parenting duties she juggles. She's a recent transplant to the area, like so many who live in Arizona. As a result of her husband's job, she's moved from New Jersey. She likes it here, but prefers the East Coast and misses family and their old lifestyle.

Her point about being outnumbered isn't lost on me. Prior to Enrique's arrival, there were many times that I wondered if I should stop at one. It took several years for me to understand that Miguel will face his emotional challenges for a lifetime, and his wounds, a result of abandonment and neglect, will never fully mend, regardless of how much love I provide him. For so long, I thought Miguel was angry because I was doing something wrong. I felt defeated when he became incensed and yelled he hated me. I thought this behavior was normal—normal that a small child would regularly resist love and find so much satisfaction in defiance. The realization that this was the result of what happened before me was painful but a huge relief. This clarity only came once Enrique arrived.

At some level, Miguel and I were never a complete family. I feel guilty saying this but I can't imagine him without a sibling. Having two older brothers and knowing how important they are in my adult life, I wanted Miguel to have the same feeling of acceptance and connectedness. I see this same connection in Miguel on those few occasions when he's reunited with his half-brother, Javier. A sibling has the potential to provide a deep bond that lasts well beyond a parent's lifetime. Miguel has always struggled with authority and at times it makes parenting nearly impossible. A brother's love and the potential for a lifelong connection come without the negative connotation of authority.

The fact that Enrique is laid-back and tranquil made it easy for Miguel to welcome his younger brother. At this Guatemalan gathering, there is a backyard teeming with children just like him, with sweet and gentle dispositions. Upon his arrival, Enrique imbued a simplicity and equilibrium to our lives that brought Miguel and me closer. From all accounts, Miguel wants to be a good big brother to Enrique, and as for Enrique, he appears to be grateful to finally have a family.

The host for today's party is an unmarried physician who has adopted several Asian girls and more recently a young son from Guatemala. As a fellow single parent, I enjoy talking with her. She guides me through the recent renovation of her ranch house, which includes an additional bedroom and another bathroom in which several teenage girls crowd in front of the mirror applying make-up and arranging their hair. We talk in the kitchen among the remains of lunch—a submarine sandwich, a few remaining potato chips and a handful of chocolate chip cookies—scattered on the kitchen table. A half dozen or so liters of soda are open on the counter. The spilled remains of several of them create a funny squeaking noise as shrieking children run continuously through the kitchen. The two of us talk about our challenges raising our oldest children, both of whom appear to struggle with oppositional issues. "It's easy to overlook the compliant ones." I feel uncomfortable admitting that I spend much more time managing Miguel's outbursts than nurturing my new son, but it's true. I share a difficult incident that happened just yesterday. Miguel tore off the bottom hinge off his bedroom door during a tirade. The meltdown occurred because I asked him to pick up his tools from a messy woodworking project in the garage. After he refused to stop and clean up, I sent him to timeout. I spent the afternoon dealing with outbursts, anger, and a broken door. "Enrique is self-reliant and disappears, playing in his room during these meltdowns. It's not fair to him, but we deal as best we can." I get the feeling she can relate, as she nods supportively.

It will be months before we meet again. The party ends with a photo of all the children. Parents beg their children to stay put so more adults can grab their cameras and take photos. Enrique is held like a hotdog, high over the heads of several of the older boys. He laughs uncontrollably.

Our family is falling into place, and in no small part due to Rosa. Routine defines most days. With almost two years under her belt, she has the longest tenure of any of the nannies. She and her family are now an extension of our own. She's excited because her husband, Armando, will soon move to Phoenix. They're planning to rent an apartment in the same complex as Alejandra, and will be within walking distance of the house. Armando's move brings them one step closer to uniting their family. This leaves only Carolina, Rosa's youngest daughter, in Mexico. Rosa talks of Carolina potentially moving to Arizona in the next year after her boyfriend finishes law school. Several times a week, Rosa babysits her grandchildren at our house. Daniela and Francisco play harmoniously with Miguel and Enrique, and to a stranger's eye, it would be impossible to identify which are not Rosa's grandchildren.

More than nanny, Rosa has evolved into a combination of mother and grandmother. Although I carry out many of the same tasks, she does them better. Each morning, Enrique allows Rosa to pluck him from bed, and carry him to the kitchen table to eat breakfast alongside his brother. She kisses him numerous times before setting him down. Enrique has recently started attending Koala Care, a preschool attached to Miguel's elementary school, just blocks from our house. Each morning, Rosa walks with Miguel and pushes Enrique in a three wheel jogger. This will be the routine until Enrique's legs grow stronger and he can walk the distance on his own. With the help of friends and teachers, Enrique is learning more English every day, and can sing the ABCs. At times, he confuses English words as I do my best to decipher what he's trying to say. One night he was insistent that he wanted an "ocean" before he went to bed. He was frustrated because I didn't understand him, and it wasn't until I saw his big brother eating ice cubes that I realized he was thirsty and wanted what his brother had. After preschool, Enrique plays with Daniela and enjoys racing his tricycle down the incline driveway, around the cul-de-sac, and back again. Miguel continues to parade his brother around the block like a new puppy, in the Red Flyer wagon we bought at a neighbor's garage sale.

Our lives are much the same as other families in the neighborhood. I volunteer in Miguel's class several times a month and along with other parents, I grade papers, staple homework assignments, and work in the teachers' lounge on special projects. On other occasions, I help Miguel and his classmates in his group for struggling readers. I supervise kickball or the food line to ensure there's no rough-housing or food fights. On these days, I eat cafeteria food with Miguel and his buddies at a picnic table in the shade. As the coach of his Little League team, I know many of Miguel's classmates and their parents who sit around us, several of whom are also in his Cub Scout den.

Most Sundays, we attend mass led by Franciscan priests. The Franciscans have created an open and accepting community that attracts a diverse group of members from across Phoenix. This includes a large number of gay parishioners, both single and partnered, who come because they know they're welcome. The message is one of inclusion, very different from our neighborhood church, which has been run by a series of pastors who support a bishop that espouses a return to "strong family values" and traditions that predate Vatican II.

Faith grounds me and gives me a sense of purpose that I feel compelled to pass on to my children. Much of the angst and lack of direction that I see in young people comes from a lack of worth and self-respect. Some may question my choice to raise my boys Catholic given the church's stance on gays and a long list of past wrongdoings. However, with any established religion comes a struggle and disagreement over theology and hierarchy, and in the end, it's all about a personal relationship with your creator that carries the day. My direct relationship with God is separate from organized religion and is a fundamental lesson I learned from my parents as a young boy.

One of my most defining childhood memories is of my mom driving up to the rectory, the home of our parish priest, and positioning the car so my window was in clear earshot of her conversation. She waited until confession was over and the priest had time to return home. After summoning him to the front door, she preceded to ball him out for making my return to confession difficult and embarrassing. "How dare you humiliate a child who actually wants to go to confession?" She went on to suggest he should be rewarding me for being one of the few Catholics who actually returned to communion during the Lenten season.

I believe life involves a higher source: one much greater than ourselves. I share this belief with my young sons. I'm not sold on the belief that they must grow up Catholic to experience salvation, but rather need to respect themselves, others, and their creator. Catholicism is a means to instill these lessons and can be done similarly with or without the hundreds of other religious institutions around the world. Live by The Golden Rule, regardless of faith—as my parents always taught – and you will be good to go. Religion provides a discipline and structure that is helpful to ensure these principles are instilled at a young age and not forgotten or lost. With all that competes for our time, its structure ensures we reflect each week to reinforce these fundamental beliefs.

Once a month I volunteer in my boys' religious education classes, which includes about a dozen two to nine year-olds. I use the term "teach" loosely; usually, I play a simple game or supervise a craft project which highlights themes of sharing, love, and friendship. My favorite activity is taking the children on a nature walk through the garden as we talk about the amazing creations on earth. As the children walk, they point to flowers, oranges, and rabbits that run throughout the grounds.

With Enrique's adoption complete, I begin the process of coming out to remaining family and friends, as well as in my workplace. For years I held this more public declaration off while I worked my way through two very lengthy adoptions, fearful that my sexuality would jeopardize this process. Acknowledging that I am gay turned out to be much less of a shock to family and friends and more a confirmation for many, but it felt good nonetheless to clear the air and finally be honest. There's a sense of empowerment and freedom that comes with this disclosure and as a result I decide to dip my feet into the dating world once again by placing several classified ads in a local alternative newspaper. This is well before social networking sites dominated matchmaking and still required a recorded message and the creation of a voice mailbox.

Rosa watches the kids as I meet the first of several guys in a coffee shop. I am confused as to why he would bring a large photo album of a recent trip to Africa. Looking through photos can be awkward for family, but insisting a guy you just met go through pages of them is just plain odd. He is nervous, sweats a lot, and refers to his friends and travel-mates as "the girls." He tells me we can stop at any time but when I try to steer the conversation clear from Africa, he insists on continuing. I curse myself for not picking up cues earlier that this guy is crazy and exit abruptly as he talks of an upcoming trip to Greece. He is just one in a series of nutty first and only dates. Although unsuccessful, they help me appreciate this will be a slow process and one that has to fit around my ultimate priority: my kids.

At such young ages, my boys don't know their father is gay or even what the word means. Although they hear other kids use the words "gay" or "fag," shouted on the school playground, they have no real context to ground these terms. After so many years and much change, it's amazing how words are still used to injure. As a single gay parent, living in a suburban Phoenix neighborhood, it's clearly a long way from living in Los Angeles or New York. I'm navigating new water and have few role models. Miguel and Enrique are two of just several handfuls of Hispanic students who attend their public elementary school. They live with a white single father in a neighborhood of two-parent Caucasian families. I'm sensitive to all these differences and struggle with how and when it's best to tell them I'm gay. Having lived in LA for more than a decade, I miss the diversity of a larger city, and the broader acceptance. However, I can't imagine raising my boys there, given the challenges that come with living in such a large urban setting.

I consult several child psychologists all of whom suggest allowing them to take the lead and ask questions; when they're ready, I should provide them with age appropriate answers. I make the decision to go with this strategy. Although I don't tell the boys that I'm gay, I also don't give them the impression I will ever get married. At times, this decision leads me to re-examine the strategy.

I participate in a soccer carpool with several parents of Miguel's teammates. One of the boys, a redheaded kid who is hyper and talkative, leans his head out the window and begins yelling "Fag… fag" at the top of his lungs at a driver of a car who tries to change lanes and almost runs us off the road. "Randall…enough," I shout in the direction of the backseat. The other boys are laughing. "Using fag is not appropriate," I attempt to counsel the group of them on political correctness. I ask them if they know what the word means. Randall, who is nine and a year older than the others, says "It's when two men suck each other's dicks." I am stunned and at a loss for words. I toss and turn that night, unable to sleep. I contemplate whether to call Randall's parents in the morning and let them know about our conversation. Having met Randall's father, I am certain this lesson came from him. Randall basically told me as much on the drive home. I shudder to think about what else this father is teaching him.

After a long and restless night, I decide not to say a word, fearful this will come back to harm my boys.

NINETEEN

Wanted: Co-Pilot

Before losing my job, I make the difficult decision to sell my house. I'm a causality of a merger between two large homebuilders. Unwilling to relocate, I'm determined to stretch a small severance package until I can find another job. Still owing money on the 401K loan that I took out to cover Enrique's adoption, times are tenuous. The pressure to provide for my two boys weighs heavy and stresses me out. Prior to the move, we hold a monster garage sale to pare down our possessions to fit into our new condo. The night before the sale my brother Kevin slashes prices on many of my handmade price tags, and prepares me for the reality check I will face in the morning. "Get ready to bargain," he says.

This is my first official garage sale. Miguel and Enrique are excited because they have several of their possessions for sale and I've told them they can keep the proceeds from any of the items they sell. Willingly, they select much of the junk which has piled up in their closets. Parting with these toys is a must, given our impending downsizing.

At 5:30 a.m., Miguel and I begin moving furniture out from the garage and line it along the sidewalk. Soon after, my mom pulls up with bagels and is ready to pitch in. Enrique is sound asleep as the first bargain hunters begin showing up well before sun-up. The large dining room set and several pairs of the boys' jeans are first

WANTED: CO-PILOT | 163

to go. Most of the earliest shoppers are Hispanic families who are looking to purchase basic necessities. After several hours, the majority of my belongings are gone. What once filled a four-bedroom house has been negotiated and sold in the blink of an eye. Near the end of a very long morning, an older woman with disheveled gray hair and a very large rear-end packed into black stretch pants approaches with one of the few remaining items in her hands. "I'm a school teacher," she says to me, "and as you know we don't make much money. Would you take fifty cents for these puzzles?" The woman shakes the large box full of games with a retail value of at least $50, wanting to negotiate down from one dollar to fifty cents. "The pieces are all here, aren't they?" she asks, concerned she might not be getting a fair deal. The woman before me is the only customer left after a morning full of haggling over nickels and dimes. I find everything about her distasteful. I yearn to spew a list of responses. "At least you make money; I've lost my job and have been forced to sell my house and most of my belongings. Did I mention I have two small children?" Rather than engage the unpleasant woman before me, I choose to say nothing. "Honey, I'll take care of her," my mom jumps up from her chair, afraid of what I might say in a moment of weakness and exhaustion. I turn and walk into the nearly empty house. Putting distance between me and this last negotiation proves to be a better option than melting down in front of the snarky school teacher.

Aimlessly I meander through the boys' bedrooms. I open their vacated closets and feel sorry for myself. I close my bedroom door and sit alone on the floor. I feel disoriented and anxious as I look at the carpet indentation, which is the only remnant of the king-size bed that once anchored the spacious room.

We move into the two-story 1,100 square foot condo that I've purchased across the street from the boys' school, just a few short blocks from our previous home. Our new neighbors are elderly single women, divorced mothers with children, and young adults who sometimes party late into the night. I'm operating in survival mode and making important decisions in a quick and raw fashion.

My concerns about my overdrawn 401K account and unemployment are constants and give me plenty of reason to obsess and fret. With the downsizing, I'm left little choice but to make the most difficult decision: Rosa can no longer be our nanny. This means she'll need to find another job to support her family. Having her step out of the boys' lives so abruptly will be another difficult transition for them, a huge and meaningful disruption, not to mention the struggles of my own that I anticipate with her absence. She, like Paulina, Carmen, and Ana before her, brought balance, continuity, and joy to each new day.

Rosa follows a familiar strategy of answering a newspaper ad in the "Domestic" section of the classifieds. I provide a glowing reference: "You'd be crazy not to hire her," I say to the anxious mother of two small girls on the other end. She has a long list of important questions, most of which I failed to ask years earlier. "You won't regret it," I assure her before ending our call. Hours later, I repeat similar positive comments to the woman's husband, who is calling to put his fears at bay. And with that, Rosa is gone; no longer a daily part of our lives.

If I find myself in a pinch, Rosa suggests her husband, Armando, can babysit. More or less retired, he's always looking to earn extra money for his family. Most days, the boys will go to Koala Care, the pre-school Enrique attended that also offers an after-school daycare program. On days when it's closed, Armando may be a good option but with money tight, I will have to play this by ear. I struggle as a part-time independent contractor, working in marketing to piecemeal enough hours to cover our monthly expenses. Frozen orange juice concentrate and generic bread are our new reality. Big Lots and dollar stores are my newfound friends.

My boys and I literally live on top of one another. My bedroom is directly above theirs, and while this is difficult for everyone, the tiny space hits Miguel hardest. Forced into the small confines of the condo, he often sounds like a caged animal: fiercely rebellious and easily agitated. Change is not his friend and the move has triggered behaviors that I hoped were well in our past. Although we all miss the large grassy front yard, the lack of movement is hardest on him. He's not a "nester" or one to sit for any amount of time with a book in hand or watch television. He must be on the move. With no garage or tools to call his own, Miguel is a fish out of water. He's in desperate need of space. Our condo provides little of this, and as a result he's clearly beside himself, which provokes defiance and opposition to most things.

At times, it all becomes too painful – too sad. Quiet finally settles upon our small condo at the end of a meltdown, and turbulence is temporarily at rest. I need to share the bedlam. "It was a bad one," I say to Jake, who unexpectedly came into my life just a few months ago. I don't dare say too much, for fear of scaring him away. On nightly phone calls, Jake consoles me. Like clockwork, once the sun rises and the despair finally dissipates, I regroup for another day.

On the other hand, transition has once again come easily to Enrique; it always has. Change appears to roll off his tiny shoulders. He's most comfortable in small spaces, and his favorite spot is his bed on the top bunk, which affords almost coffin-like movement between ceiling and mattress. I marvel at the differences between the two, no more so than how each boy has handled the move. With Miguel now ten years old and his brother seven, there can be no discounting how both are reacting to the long list of changes. Once again, it reminds me just how significant those first few years of life are as they relate to a child's long term well-being.

I whisper while lying completely still, afraid to move. My bed is positioned directly above the boys' room and I do everything in my power not to budge. Any disturbance sends creaks through the floorboards which reverberate below and risks a potential awakening. At the moment, Miguel sleeps, which holds his angst at bay. Randomly, he yells out from his restlessness in an effort to exfoliate distant memories. Our move and the resulting changes unleash his past. Although we've not reverted to the beginning, we have taken several giants steps backward. Progress due to stability and love slips away; volatility takes its place. Listening to the occasional disparate scream is eerie and heartbreaking.

"Remind me why you're still here?" I ask Jake bluntly. On this night, the question is as much for me as it is for him. However, tonight I need to hear him say it. "Because I love you," he states unwaveringly. "He's just so angry and sad." I can formulate no real explanation for my oldest son's outbursts. Since our move, I've tried everything to console him but he's now spiraling out of control. "He was on the top step crying, screaming out—for no apparent reason—he sounds like he's in complete agony." Jake remains silent. "How can a fourth grader be so sad?" He chooses not to answer this impossible and rhetorical question. The streetlight positioned directly outside my window floods through the cheap Home Depot shade hanging slightly crookedly above it. The brightness frustrates me but at some level I'm grateful not to face the darkness.

"So, what happened?" Jake asks after a long silence. "How did it start?" We live across from the pool and Jacuzzi that anchors the small complex. The neighborhood park is just blocks away and the boys' school is directly across the street. Although this is familiar territory, Miguel misses home. "He refused to do his homework and began tearing the pages out of his math book. He threw it against the wall over and over again and finally broke the vase on the hall table." Jake is quiet. Running out the front door, Miguel shouted, "I hate you. I'm running away." Then he stood in the courtyard screaming "I hate you" repeatedly. He slammed the rod-iron fence loudly, before running down the street. Since moving in, Miguel has performed a similar show for neighbors several times a week.

In a landscape ravine, I retrieved Miguel from his hiding place and picked him up. In darkness, he kicked and screamed down the streets of our little buttoned-down complex. "I hate you," he continued to shriek. As I passed the neighboring condos, I heard doors open and close. It was cold and fortunately the street was empty and dark, lit only by the occasional street lamp.

"I feel trapped," I tell Jake once I finish the story. Living in such a small place gives us few opportunities to escape one another. Enrique has a classmate who lives next store. Wisely, he spends much of his time there in an effort to avoid the nightly drama. After dinner, I encourage the boys to bike or rollerblade with me to the nearby park in an effort to burn off excessive energy, with the hope of reducing meltdowns.

Jake and I met in a gay softball league. Twelve gay men and one lesbian make up the roster of the Pirates, although informally we refer to ourselves as the Bad News Bears. We are sponsored by a hole-in-the-wall windowless bar called Pumphouse II, which the two of us have yet to visit but teammates tell us features weekend drag shows. Jake is the pitcher; I play shortstop. We have few other teammates who can successfully throw the ball overhand from third to first base. Our games are held Sunday mornings at Cesar Chavez High School in South Phoenix. Over my shoulder, I lug a large bag full of games and sports equipment to ensure the boys remain engaged and out of trouble. I spend most innings with one eye on the ball, the other on the two of them. There are emergency time outs to break up brotherly spats and regular redirection away from a gang of affectionate cheerleaders dressed in drag. My teammates pay special attention to watching over the boys while making herculean efforts to curb discussions of their Saturday night adventures.

Unbeknownst to me, Jake's friends come to the game to check me out. A single dad with two rambunctious kids, they're eager to weigh in on Jake's new love interest. They sit casually among the small group of spectators and watch me as I repeatedly shepherd the boys back to the dugout. They appear most concerned about my fashion sense, or lack thereof, asking Jake after the game, "Why does he wear dark-colored socks with low cut hiking boots in a softball game?"

Many of our competitors played baseball in high school and some in college, and they put us to shame quickly and painfully. We lose every game during the season except the final one which we win by forfeit. There remain unconfirmed reports that our opponents, who are undefeated, didn't think it was worth their time to turn out for the final game. We claim victory and afterward celebrate at our home bar.

Prior to the softball season, I'm not certain a life partner is in my cards. Truly, who would want to step into my world? I'm far from a hot commodity in the gay community. As a single dad in his late thirties, dealing with the aftermath of a corporate downsizing, I have a number of strikes against me. My days are spent tending to the needs of my children rather than tending bar. I'm more focused on finding my next job than my next date. Miguel is on my mind, constantly.

"Kids make me nervous," Jake discloses during our first date at Applebee's. I live some thirty miles away but claim to be in the neighborhood to pull off this first meeting. Despite myself, I laugh at his confession. "Kids make every parent nervous…don't worry about it." I attempt to downplay his concern and work to regain my composure. "I've never been good at talking with kids…they make me uncomfortable." Jake is logical and analytical. His low key demeanor is a contrast to my boys' unbridled spontaneity, and yet I understand his discomfort. He's never contemplated parenthood and makes a point of reiterating that several times. His own childhood was modest and humble. He grew up in a single-wide mobile home in Paducah, Kentucky, raised by a stern but loving single mom, more or less as an only child. Although he had an older brother who was raised by his father, the two lived very separate lives.

Jake is gentle and honest. By any standard, gay or straight, he's good-looking. His quiet personality is appealing and I find myself immediately attracted to his genuine sincerity. We make plans to hike Camelback Mountain the day after Thanksgiving and are both excited at the potential prospect of a budding relationship.

Jake and I are an unlikely match, however, we complement one another nicely. He's technical and analytical; I am spontaneous and emotional. He is introspective while I'm vocal and outgoing. He likes science fiction; I like pop culture. His favorite group is Primus, mine is The Frey. He's curious and practical, I'm organized and a perfectionist. He's good at math and I'm not. He is a Libertarian at heart but claims Independent status; I'm a Democrat. However, from our modest upbringings, we share a common life perspective. We're caring and compassionate, and both have a drive to help others. I'm beguiled by his patience and kindness. Although we enjoy different activities, we both like to try new things. We love the outdoors and hike local mountains whenever we get an opportunity. Above all, he has quickly become my anchor, which keeps me grounded through my parenting struggles.

Several weeks into our "official" relationship, Jake's in a near panic. I'm on the verge of leaving the house to run to the neighborhood convenience store for milk. "How long will you be gone?" he asks in a shaky voice, poorly disguising his nervousness. "Ten minutes—I promise no more than ten." I hold back laughter on the way out the door. "Call my cell if anything happens. I believe in you!" I yell back just before the door slams closed. Why these new chaotic disruptions in Jake's once peaceful life do not scare him away remains one of life's great mysteries.

Weeks later, I cook dinner on New Year's Eve for Jake and the boys. I've changed the clocks several hours to make sure both Miguel and Enrique are in bed well before midnight. "You're going to lie to them about the start of the New Year?" Jake asks, both amused and appalled. "Absolutely," I say smiling at him. "There's no way I am going to deal with the wrath of two grouchy boys with little sleep...no harm—no foul!" As the clock strikes 10:00 p.m. in Arizona, we watch the ball drop from Times Square and celebrate on the black pavement in front of the condo. The boys and I bang pots and pans with big metal spoons. Miguel and Enrique are unable to convince Jake to take up noise making. He's shy and looks worried that our neighbors won't like our loud celebration. His embarrassment only makes him more attractive. More importantly, his arrival on the eve of this New Year is nothing short of divine intervention.

With the exception of Jake, our transition remains grueling. I miss Rosa, who was as much a caregiver for me as for my boys. In fact, it isn't until I see her in Target with the two little girls she now babysits that I feel alone. Prior to this, but somehow like New Year's, I thought that I could reset the clock and bring her back into focus, and into our family portrait. In short order, I would land another job, make a call, and we'd be reunited. Among the many rows of Hallmark cards, Rosa smothers the boys with kisses. Now a bit older, they half-heartedly attempt to push away her blatant and explicit affections, but quickly and unconditionally surrender within her all-encompassing embrace.

Rosa and her family surrounded us with a veil of normality and acceptance. Repetition was everything and without her we remain out-of-sorts. Her mere presence brought a sense of assurance when things were out of control. The familiar smell of her perfume and her unconditional love were a natural balm for a household of boys. Enrique became a fixture in her lap, energized by her loving touch. Miguel was calmed by her motherly embrace. In her presence, I found patience. Now, seeing her unexpectedly babysitting the small girls, it feels inevitable and final. The boys are older and independent enough to make it through this critical juncture, but now it is up to me to carry the day.

Flying solo is a bold choice. Navigating parenting without a partner can be overwhelming. More than ever, I realize my nannies buffered me from many of these realities. For most single parents, there are no safety nets or severance packages, leaving only the daily struggle to feed and shelter their children. There are no timeouts, sounding boards, or scheduled breaks to regroup physically or emotionally. Equilibrium comes solely from an inner strength and fortitude. With limited options, right choices can still be made. With few exceptions, it involves sacrifice and a complete commitment to the betterment of children.

TWENTY

Phantom Oasis

The boys race down the stairs and through the white sand. With the sliding glass doors open, the cool ocean breeze fills the cavernous living room. The sky is blue and the water green and lightly choppy. Miguel and Enrique quickly reach the ocean's edge and jump over waves to join a man who's bent over and intently looking through the surf. Once spotty and sparsely developed, this stretch of Mexican beach is now fully lined with elaborate new buildings. The large white adobe structure with the circular dome is the first of many behind the gates manned by an uninterested security guard. The home, located several hours south of the Arizona border, belongs to friends who've invited us to stay during the boys' spring vacation.

The entrance to the house has wooden gates that must first be unlocked and wheeled open. A small compound unfolds as we drive the car forward. To the right, a two-story guest house is under construction. Just beyond the property line sits a small, modest aquarium run by the local technical high school. On the other side of the sprawling main house, neighbors have a large, box-like two story stucco house with windows that open to the expansive sea. As we enter through the front door, the ocean is visible from all rooms. The white cement and adobe brick walls look and feel sturdy; orange Mexican Saltillo tile wraps throughout each room.

The centerpiece of the house is the large wooden dome ceiling that stretches over the living room and kitchen. Looking upward, Jake and I marvel at the architectural achievement. The beach runs eternally from either end of the large outdoor deck. We both take note of the fire pit and the stack of wood next to it. Several Adirondack chairs encircle the pit, inviting our return after sundown.

"Wow, what a view," Jake says, focusing outward. We stand quiet for some time while looking at Miguel and Enrique, their bodies engaged in the ocean current. The warm sun and cool breeze anchor us and overlay an immediate appreciation of this place. It's not yet summer, so humidity and jelly fish are yet to surface. A carload of supplies and rations will wait as we watch the boys trail in the wake of the lanky man. Though only hours from Phoenix, the Mexican surf is a mesmerizing contrast to the harsh, if not often lush, Sonoran Desert.

The beach is nearly empty but much further down the shore I make out several families but little else amidst the palate of white sand and greenish sea. "A bucket, a bucket…I need a bucket," Miguel races by me and grabs a large yellow one just inside the open sliding glass door. "I found one," he yells back in the direction of the ocean as Jake and I smile at one another. He frantically waves the bucket overhead, as he runs back in the direction of his brother and the mysterious man who both continue their search in the shallow rocky waters.

"If you're lucky you'll meet the Octopus Man," our friends tell us when we stop by their home in Phoenix to pick up the keys and get directions. "He's often in front of our place collecting octopus to sell to local restaurants." The boys have apparently struck gold. The man does indeed appear to be on duty, and from what we gather he looks to be giving the boys a sea critter. Miguel and Enrique have been in Rocky Point for less than thirty minutes and they have in their possession a small octopus that swims slowly around the bottom of the yellow bucket. From the expressions on their faces, I'm not sure life gets much better than this.

"He wanted us to have it," Miguel says quickly as the lumbering man walks away from the house and down the beach. "I told him thank you." Miguel's chatter is meant to counter his father's disapproving look. I've seen this strategy many times before. He's too young to understand that he has likely taken a man's livelihood and placed it in a small yellow bucket to serve as a temporary pet. But the act of kindness is touching. "What does an octopus eat?" I ask, resigned to let the boys keep the slithering gift.

Rather than having it sit vacant, my friends have generously offered up their place several times in the past, insistent we stay and enjoy the oceanfront setting. Each time I thanked them but declined, telling them I needed to make sure I had all of Enrique's adoption paperwork in place. I fear crossing the Mexican border with two small Hispanic boys in the backseat. It seems reasonable that border guards might confuse our nontraditional family as something potentially sinister. It seems plausible that one of them might ask what Jake and I are doing taking them out of the country, or back in for that matter. It took several years, but with Enrique's U.S. passport now in hand, we were ready for our maiden journey.

Prior to our trip, I peppered the boys with hypothetical questions border agents might ask, and quizzed them on appropriate responses. "What's your name?" "Who are your parents?" "Where do you live?" "Where are you going?" These impromptu role playing exercises gave me a sense of comfort but did little for the boys who thought the questions were funny. "We don't know the weirdo in the front seat," Miguel said, which made his younger brother laugh. Although there are regular stories of drug trafficking and increased crime and violence across the border region, Rocky Point has reported few such incidents and none involving American tourists. Nonetheless, the news reports redirect enough visitors away to San Diego for Spring Break, leaving the beaches of Rocky Point quiet and practically our own.

The beach house is less than a mile from the trailer park where my family camped when I was a child, nearly forty years ago. The contrast in setting between the spacious oceanside retreat and the modest trailer park is striking. This is the same beach where my brothers and I rolled out our sleeping bags and slept to the sounds of waves crashing against the shore, and where we lit firecrackers at night in front of a large audience of fellow campers. My parents and I would take long walks on this beach and admire the sprawling homes built by Americans. We walked for what felt like miles before encountering small clusters of these oceanfront getaways. Now, within the gated community, almost every lot is developed.

This is Jake's first visit to Rocky Point and our first international family trip. Things are good after two years together. I recently found another job and am searching for a home to buy in our same neighborhood. The vacation comes at a perfect time to retool for what feels like a new life waiting our return. The boys still know Jake as their dad's "friend" and it will be several more years before they fully understand the term "partner." We've decidedly taken it slowly to give the boys time to grow comfortable with Jake and allow them a better perspective to address the likely taunts they may face from schoolmates, who want to make an issue out of their gay father and his partner.

The boys like Jake and are excited he's come along. He serves as a good buffer between my role as father and disciplinarian. A positive and supportive adult, he's also a good listener when one of the boys is upset. He's come a long way and grows more and more confident in his communication with them. Although children were never part of his plan, his seamless inclusion within our family has given him an important role in which he regularly makes a clear and meaningful contribution. He experiences love from the two boys in a way that adds meaning not only to his life but ours as well.

In the morning, we leave the compound, as we refer to it, and head into town for a scheduled ocean outing. Far in the distance we can see them stacked one on top of the other—large condos that appear on the horizon like a mirage. We glide in a catamaran that is operated by an American who has moved to Rocky Point with his wife. In their fifties, the two offer sailing excursions for tourists.

The captain's wife highly recommends the two-hour trip in and around the waters of Cholla Bay. "It's a kid pleaser," she assures me.

Our friends have told us the captain has cancer, but I see no signs of it. Standing behind the large stainless steel wheel, he looks tan and relaxed; perhaps his laid back lifestyle has placed the disease in remission. He's semi-retired and living a dream. Jovial and free spirited, he employs two young Mexican deckhands, who remain busy setting sails and serving Coronas to the dozen or so guests on-board. Miguel and Enrique are bent over the bow with their hands trailing the waters as the boat effortlessly glides through the port. Their small necks are lost within two red adult-sized life preservers as they're on the lookout for dolphin. The quiet port is very much what I remember from my own childhood. Many of the architectural landmarks that dot the downtown area remain unchanged. We move slowly past stationary shrimp boats anchored along the very same docks from which my parents bought fish years earlier. Soon Jim has the nimble sail boat moving freely in the open waters.

As the wind increases the boat's speed, I turn my baseball cap backward. The sky is wide-open and blue. Drinking a beer, my face feels flush and suddenly it happens, quicker, much quicker than usual. I have one of those fleeting moments when I want to spontaneously relocate myself and my family from our suburban, big box existence to a beach destination. I refer to these times as my "Jimmy Buffet" moments. And why not? I'm miles from the noisy intersection that sits in front of our neighborhood Target, Famous Footwear, and Chili's. Out on the horizon, I see no blinking Supercuts sign. I've been transported to paradise and all is good at this moment. Calm overruns any repressed anxiety or worries about our visit to a foreign country. Jake's eyes are closed; I see them behind his sunglasses. His face is pointed to the sun and I feel like I have a clear view into his soul. From the sheer joy that comes from the warmth of the sun, he smiles slightly. He looks handsome and tan. Our arms touch as we lean back to maximize the sun exposure. The boys laugh as they splash one another. Everyone is content. This is one of those rare moments when everyone is happy and I want to fully treasure it.

We need only ask for *mas cervezas* and we will be served, Jim reminds us. He talks with an older couple from Tucson about his move to Rocky Point, the history of the place, and his fondness for the local people. You can see envy in the eyes of the other passengers as he laughs freely. Who wouldn't want to spend their days on the ocean?

Jim instructs the sails be turned and the boat quickly rights itself in the direction of Sandy Beach. As the boat parallels the long white strip of sand, they're unmistakable once again. Aligned like dominos, there are a half dozen or so large condo towers huddled along the beach. Once filled with travel trailers and tents, the view looks like a modified postcard from Acapulco or Puerto Vallarta.

We sail in front of the mammoth contemporary towers and decipher elaborate pools, tented cabanas, and long stretches of private beach, which appear nearly vacant. There's a green golf course in the far distance that snakes beyond the massive developments. The large condo buildings have countless balconies that all look out upon the vast sea, as if desperate for sunlight to further pollinate them. Off the right bow are several parasails that dot the sky, while two jet skiers rumble in circles not far behind us. A fast moving motor boat tows a group of tourists on what looks like a yellow inflated hotdog that cuts the surf and passes us. After a quick maneuver, the small crowd is dumped into the chilly ocean water. The passengers laugh nervously as they wait for the boat and yellow inflatable to circle back and pluck them to safety. Jim directs the deckhands to again adjust the sails, which redirects the boat back in the direction of town. The immense towers quickly shrink in the distance as our excursion nears an end.

Soon after, we follow large billboards along the main drag that direct us down an unimproved dirt road. The modern signage promises nothing less than paradise. I'm determined to visit the mecca of high rise buildings we saw from the boat, needing to confirm that it wasn't merely a phantom oasis induced by Coronas and the warm sun. The wealth supporting such a lifestyle is in complete contrast to everything I remember of Rocky Point.

The wind has since picked up. The few cars in front of us create a dust storm that blankets the rickety shacks that balance along the road, as a pack of gangly dogs runs alongside our car. The irony of our journey nearly forces me to retreat. We're headed to a promised land of condos and luxury amenities, but must first pass impoverished living conditions that are reminiscent of a third world refugee camp. Part of me is compelled to return to the safety of the compound until I remind myself of the complete hypocrisy. The shacks made of plywood, metal, and tar paper provide little respite from the driving wind. Indeed there are brick and mortar structures along the way, but even these buildings look like they'd collapse under a strong current. The shear lack of vegetation is depressing, yet children play in front of several of the homes. As I look at my boys in the backseat, they're engaged in hand-held video games, oblivious to the children playing and the passing poverty. "It would really be difficult living here, wouldn't it guys?" I make a feeble attempt to draw them back into reality.

The road is wide but filled with craters and bumps, and as a result we make slow progress. The tepid speed highlights the desperation and gravity of the residents' plight. The occasional billboard, rising well above the primitive structures, features smiling Anglos with golf clubs in hand on a lush green golf course. No doubt these signs are positioned strategically to refocus the faint of heart. I feel uncomfortable as we drive onward to our posh destination and can't imagine the angst that comes from purchasing one of these beachfront units and regularly reckoning with such explicit poverty.

A guardhouse appears as the squalor dissipates. A friendly man directs us in English down a long and winding grassy marketing trail with beautiful plants designed to excite potential buyers, while at the same time attempting to soften concerns of the overwhelming despair that sits just beyond the property line. We end up in front of a series of large towers. Beyond them are several other incomplete residential high rise structures that dot the beach.

Wanting to avoid a hard sell presentation, we quickly pass through the sleek marble lobby, greeting the professionally dressed women at the front counter. With a snappy *"Hola,"* I signal Jake and the kids to exit through sliding glass doors, pretending to know our final destination. A huge swimming pool lies before us; encircling it are high rise towers, their reflection illuminated in the blue water. Beyond the pool, the choppy ocean rolls in. There's a large bar to the right of us at the pool's edge and more around the perimeter. Although it's Spring Break, the place is nearly empty. There are seemingly hundreds of lounge chairs and numerous cabanas that would be enticing if not for the wind that hammers us with an unforgiving clip.

Back through the lobby we beeline for the elevators to get a better look higher up in the towers. The boys fight to push the many elevator buttons, so we end up stopping many times before exiting at one of the floors near the top of the building. We find ourselves on a balcony looking out onto the sea and the massive pool far below. In all directions, there are few residents or tourists to be found. The place almost feels abandoned, as if we've come after hours to the Universal Studios back lot.

The ocean, the same we sailed earlier in the day, is now a volatile mess. The parasails and oversized yellow flotation devices are nowhere to be found. On the elevator ride down, we plan our great escape and return back to our own gated community. The boys are anxious to return to the beach and catch fish, while I'm grateful for the glass of wine in my hand and the sight of Jake and my children standing near the ocean's edge.

The next morning brings bad news. The octopus has died on the deck. Apparently, he worked his way out of the bucket during the night, intent on heading back to sea. Without any water to buoy his journey, he died, encrusted to the deck. We hold a quick heave-ho burial ceremony and return him to the ocean. Soon after, we pack up and return to Phoenix.

TWENTY-ONE

Sí, Se Puede!

"*Qué Padre!*" I greet Rosa as I enter the kitchen from the garage door, pointing at the new car in the driveway. Rosa's oldest daughter, Alejandra, is teaching me to sound more "Mexican." I park my faded navy blue Ford Explorer, which has recently surpassed 100,000 miles, next to the sleek, shiny Mercedes. "Cool car," I repeat in English as I playfully jab Rosa's side for a reaction.

Alejandra has recently purchased it and Rosa is borrowing the car for the day. "*Estoy nerviosa,*" Rosa says she's nervous about driving such an expensive car. Alejandra is piecing together her interpretation of the American dream, aggressively pursuing her goals and along the way establishing a new life for herself.

Now the mother of two and the wife of a successful American construction contractor, she lives in a modern stucco house near a golf course not far from me. The home sits in a large master planned community nestled on a hillside and adjacent to the Phoenix mountain preserve. She and her husband are in the process of moving into a new, larger home near affluent shops and excellent schools. She met Phil in the Spanish class she teaches for executives who are interested in becoming bilingual. Through her marital status, Alejandra hopes to apply soon for U.S. Citizenship. Phil has made a small fortune from the Phoenix area real estate boom. He has a dry wall company that subcontracts to the many homebuilders trying to keep up with the housing demand in the many suburbs that have mushroomed seemingly overnight just outside the Phoenix city limits. With his hard work has come financial success.

We attend a swim party at Alejandra's home. A large group has gathered around the pool; Miguel and Enrique quickly jump in and join the other kids. At twelve and nine years of age respectively, the two tower over most of the other children and do cannonballs, hoping to get as many adults wet as possible. They gravitate to Francisco, Mauricio's oldest child, and Daniela, Alejandra's daughter. It's been a number of months and they're excited to see one another. Several partygoers mistake the rambunctious group as cousins. Mauricio and Gabriela now have a young daughter, Isabel, who is gripping at her father's neck in the shallow end of the pool. Mauricio keeps an eye on the kids, playing tag as he gently lowers his daughter up and down. Gabriela dangles her feet close-by.

The party is a melting pot of various cultures that now represents Rosa's extended family. There are pockets of English and Spanish spoken throughout the backyard. Near the barbeque, I meet Phil for the first time. He and several of his friends drink beer while laughing with one another. For the moment, a raging fire on the grill splits Phil's attention between his friends and the uncooked hamburgers and hot dogs that are now consumed by flames. He's self-made with definite rough edges, but appears to be in love with Alejandra.

In great detail, Phil shares the particulars of their first kiss. "Let's just say I knew I was in for more than Spanish that first time I kissed her." Alejandra is embarrassed by his not so subtle summary. My first impression of Phil is not a positive one; he appears to be an odd addition. Although Rosa and her family have struggled financially, they're proud and refined. This is Alejandra's second marriage and I'm hopeful she finds happiness. I meet Phil's two older teenage daughters, who live with his ex-wife but remain in the picture. "Okay," Alejandra smiles and shrugs as I ask her in a hushed tone how the relationship is coming with the girls.

Unmistakably, Alejandra is the glue that binds the party together. Effortlessly slipping in and out of Spanish, she works the crowd. Like her mother, she has an ease about her.

In an effort to escape the sun, Rosa and Armando sit with family members under an umbrella near the pool's edge. In Spanish, I am introduced to several relatives. Armando shouts "Marco - Polo" to the kids in the pool. As we hug, Rosa kisses me on the cheek. She smells of her elegant perfume. She and Armando have recently moved into my condo after living in several different apartments. It served as our home during a difficult transition, and now I'm excited to have the two living close by. Several months before, I purchased a house not far from our previous one after becoming successfully established with my new employer, another large homebuilder. Our new home gives us back much needed space.

The party is an opportunity to reconnect with Rosa and her family. Now that I'm once again gainfully employed, I've hired Armando to work early mornings and late afternoons. The boys are older and so I need him more as a cab driver than a nanny. Though Armando is also willing to pitch in with household chores, his primary job will be shuttling the boys between their various after-school activities. Last week we did an early morning drive past the home of Miguel's reading tutor. Frustrated that I am still unable to fully convey the directions clearly in Spanish, the two of us drive by the house at 6:45 a.m. before I leave for work.

Armando is happy to be working and to have the chance to contribute and earn money once again. From selling meat out of a cooler from his car trunk, to hawking rubber yo-yos at county fairs, he's tried his hand at several part-time jobs since moving to Phoenix. Without a green card and fluent language skills, his prospects are limited and for all practical purposes he's been retired. It has been a long road from once running a successful contracting business in Mexico. With a long list of afterschool activities, including baseball and soccer practice, as well as Scout meetings, Armando will be invaluable. To date, his favorite task is attending Little League practice. He coached his son Mauricio's baseball team for many years and relishes the time back on the field. Miguel's coach allows Armando to shag balls and participate in batting practice.

Armando works mornings from 6:30 a.m. – 8:30 a.m. and then from 2:30 p.m. – 6:00 p.m., which gives me the coverage I need for the boys before and after school. The transition doesn't come without some bumps along the way. Clearly I've been spoiled by Rosa and the other women who came before her. At some level, Armando and I are an unconventional pair. He has spent a lifetime managing construction crews and running a successful company; it's been years since his grown children were in elementary school. He was a traditional husband and father in most every way. Rosa handled the housework, cooking, and homework, while Armando was the provider and worked long hours to support the family.

"The boys need to get their homework done first before they play." I plead with Mauricio to relay this message again to his father. "I'm probably not communicating this correctly to him in Spanish," I say, attempting to hide my frustration. Rather than finish their homework or their few daily chores, the boys easily persuade Armando to allow them to play with the neighborhood kids or watch television. Over these first few months, it feels like the inmates are running the show. Most days I find Armando supervising a group of neighborhood kids in our front yard, which has once again become the gathering spot for impromptu play. He watches them from the front porch, or while sitting in his late model Oldsmobile, listening to his favorite Mexican radio station.

Mauricio serves as facilitator for several "family meetings." As I communicate my frustrations, Mauricio translates in Spanish to his father, and several misunderstandings quickly surface. Most importantly, my expectations are unrealistic. Armando is not Rosa, or Paulina for that matter, and his experiences as a parent are far different than those of my nannies, all of whom were stay-at-home mothers. Also, there appears to be a cultural difference regarding the value and importance of homework. Mauricio communicates to his father that this is non-negotiable. No matter how hard the boys attempt to persuade Armando to allow them to go outside and play, they must first complete their homework and then show it to him. There will be more late night meltdowns with Miguel over homework, and additional "family meetings" before the routine takes shape, but once it's solidified, we settle into a good place.

These meetings with Armando are important, and help both of us create more realistic expectations. To his credit, Armando quickly comes up with rewards to get the boys to finish their assignments. He uses trips to the convenience store and Walmart as opportunities to gain his desired outcome. The new arrangement is not perfect, but it's working, and the boys are better off because of it. It's got Miguel motivated and reduces the frequency of his meltdowns.

Armando's transformation in the U.S. has been remarkable. In his early sixties, he's successfully integrated into a new life; his trips with Rosa to Hermosillo are few and far between. The two only return for doctor appointments, funerals, and visits to the Mexican Consulate every six months to renew their travel visas. Both scowl whenever the subject of the Mexican economy arises. "*Mala, mala, mala,*" Armando responds when I ask how things are there. The economic situation is dire, with little prospect of changing anytime soon. Since their move, he believes their lives are infinitely better, albeit radically different.

Recently, Armando has been busy working with a realtor and attorney to sell their home in Mexico. He regularly updates me on these efforts. From what I gather, Armando has started receiving a small Social Security stipend from the Mexican government, and he hopes that with the sale of their home, they'll be able to purchase a small place in Phoenix. Both Rosa and Armando will need to work indefinitely to remain afloat financially. With skyrocketing housing prices, purchasing one is a daunting prospect for anyone, but even more so for these two. At poolside, they quiz me on the latest condition of the real estate market.

The party remains in full force. Conversation and laughing reverberate throughout the yard. Carolina talks loudly to be heard above the screams and yelps from the kids splashing in the pool.

Mauricio and Gabriela sit nearby, their youngest daughter now sleeping in her mother's arms. Much has occurred in Carolina's life since her arrival in the U.S., and our initial discussion with her mother regarding employment so many years ago. With our long history, conversation comes easily between us. It feels like a lifetime has passed since we sat in my living room and looked through the family photos album under the wall of crosses.

Like her sister, Carolina is outgoing, but she's more vulnerable. She laughs often but also has a raw, unguarded disposition. She updates me as we sit and watch the kids play in the pool, and her English is unblemished. Even without a green card and just a travel visa, she had no problem securing a job as a nanny, babysitting twin girls for a Scottsdale couple. She's bonded quickly with them and describes the girls with a mother-like pride. The pay is adequate and she earns near what she made in Mexico. More notably, she is grateful to be in the U.S. and to be reunited with her family. She's spent the last five years watching her older sister and brother forge new paths for themselves and their families. Life has treated them well and success has come from hard work and perseverance. As a result, she remains determined and optimistic.

"I'm taking a break from men for a while," Carolina says in a low voice as she leans over to me. We both laugh at her dead-pan delivery. Three months ago, she announced to her parents she was marrying a Mexican national living in Phoenix, who she'd known for a short time. Her parents were both opposed to a quick wedding. One month after her marriage, Carolina moved back home and filed for divorce. Shortly before her nuptials, she'd broken up with her long-term boyfriend from Mexico, now an attorney, whom I'd met several times during previous visits. The marriage was likely a rebound relationship. Her family lineage does not include self-pity and she's content to put this mistake behind her, move on, and remain living in the U.S.

Mauricio moves a lawn chair closer to Carolina and me as Gabriela goes into the house to put their young daughter down for a nap. He has a bright blue beach towel wrapped around his wet suit; he's eager to update me on his budding real estate career. "The market is still crazy," he says with excitement brimming in his voice. Although there are indications of trouble on the horizon a year after the peak of the real estate boom, times are still good and there remains a competitive race to buy and sell homes. Mauricio is working with investors who have money to purchase and remodel homes and then re-sell them to Hispanics, some who are here illegally. His residency status does not allow him to hold a real estate license, so his work is focused on finding buyers and overseeing construction projects. His partner is a real estate agent who legally buys and sells the properties.

Although home prices are no longer steadily rising, many first-time homebuyers are shut out of the market. However, due to the availability of creative loan programs, even to undocumented immigrants, Mauricio's business remains viable. Not far from golf courses and upscale shopping malls, Mauricio himself has bought a tract home in an affluent suburb of Phoenix, very close to my brother. Schools in the neighborhood are good and his son plays on a Little League baseball team. Like his older sister, Alejandra, Mauricio is on the path to achieve his American dream. Gabriela, a full-time homemaker, is not fluent in English but has learned key words and phrases out of necessity in order to raise two children in a predominantly white suburb. When possible, Francisco helps translate for his mother in school and in stores. The transition is hard on her, and ultimately, Gabriela would like to move back to Mexico. But she understands jobs and opportunity will keep them here for some time. During summers, she and the children travel back home for extended vacations with her parents. She uses this time to recharge for her new world order.

Shivering and dripping wet, Enrique appears at my side. He holds his hands out to show me his prune-like fingers. After an hour of swimming, they've transformed into wrinkled sticks and he is proud of this accomplishment. Rosa scoops him up in his towel and slips him comfortably into her lap. Even at nine, Enrique enjoys being held by Rosa and allows her to kiss him on both cheeks.

Soon he crawls into my lap and rests his head on my shoulder, indicating it's time to go. I coax Miguel out of the pool and we say our goodbyes among a flood of hugs and kisses.

Days later, I hurry home to catch the local evening news. Armando has requested the afternoon off because he and his family are participating in a large demonstration. Shortly my mom will be dropping the boys off. I flip between three local news stations in hopes of a recap on the demonstration. Thousands were expected to participate in an organized march from a central Phoenix park to the State Capital building. Organizers hoped for more than 50,000 participants. They gathered to oppose a growing number of anti-immigration laws that are sweeping through the Arizona State Legislature. Proposed legislation limiting access to medical care and education are two hot-button issues, but the larger concern is the potential for racial profiling that exists with the enforcement of immigration legislation. These concerns are shared by the thousands of legal Hispanic residents, as well as a large number of other Arizonans.

Fueling the march is Sheriff Joe Arpaio, who has stepped up a series of immigration sweeps throughout predominantly Hispanic neighborhoods, with a goal to arrest as many undocumented aliens as possible. Sheriff Arpaio has made illegal immigration his primary platform and holds well-orchestrated media events to showcase the outcome of such arrests. Immigration sweeps titillate the public and appear to placate the general anxiety among white residents, who fear immigration is impacting their quality of life. With a steadily declining economy, many residents are convinced undocumented workers are taking jobs from legal Americans, as well as fueling illegal drug sales and violent crime. At the end of each sweep, handcuffed Hispanics are paraded in front of news cameras. The media finds these regular events impossible to ignore. Locally, there is no one who possesses Arpaio's abilities to successfully garner as much media attention or contest his office. His opponents complain that he should focus on criminals and not hardworking illegal immigrants. The sheriff has thousands of outstanding warrants that remain unenforced, yet he remains obsessed with deporting illegal immigrants, most of whom have no criminal record.

To many, the sheriff fills an ever-present void. Without a national approach to immigration reform and enforcement, Arpaio remains boastful and fully committed to his bold initiative. His publicized sweeps only enhance his reputation as the nation's toughest sheriff, but also further alienate Arizona as the home of extremists. Polls indicate that he's the state's most popular politician. Regularly, he contemplates a run for governor.

The demonstration is the lead story. Tens of thousands turned out for the event, which was noisy, yet peaceful. At the State Capital, counter protesters shouted anti-immigration taunts but were kept at bay by the large police presence. News cameras capture the many "*Sí, Se Puede!*" signs that were hoisted above the large crowd of demonstrators. Armando and many of his family members were somewhere among the massive group. It is all a bit surreal as I survey the crowd in hopes of spotting them. From one channel to the next, I strain to recognize a familiar face. This was to be a family front—Armando, Rosa, Alejandra, Mauricio, and Carolina, along with several of their young grandchildren. Their unified participation in the demonstration feels very American and I'm proud of their involvement.

"Things must change," Armando told me in English weeks before the protest. "We are here for our families…not for crime," he said with conviction. Armando and Rosa have strategically dodged many of the new punitive legislative actions through the efforts of a burgeoning underground immigrant community. When Arizona enacted laws prohibiting the renewal of driver's licenses to non-permanent residents, the two visited a neighboring state where such laws hadn't yet been passed. When landlords would no longer write a lease agreement in their name, a family member signed for them. This family has anchored themselves in America and now refuses to return to a life of despair. They work as a collective unit to further their goals.

Far from radical, Armando and Rosa mirror my own parents' life experiences. They've worked hard raising their family and focused on being positive role models. Their children are a top priority and with this comes much sacrifice to ensure their futures hold more promise than their own. Like my parents, they were guided by their faith and a strong work ethic. They didn't have the means to attend college, but believed hard work would bring opportunity. They didn't seek handouts, but rather focused on helping others.

However, unlike my parents, they lack financial security. After a lifetime of labor, my parents are fortunate to each have a modest pension. My dad's was the result of thirty years of service at a local pipe fitter and air conditioning union. My mom's came after twenty years working as an administrative assistant within a school district. Along with Social Security and Medicare, they've always had a level of assurance that they'd be comfortable and cared for in their retirement. This allowed them to purchase a travel trailer upon retirement, and the opportunity to visit many of the fifty states. Later, like many other middle class Arizona retirees, they bought a retirement home in the cooler climate of Flagstaff, situated among the pine trees, to escape the brutal Phoenix summers. Hard work generated options, and along with it, a level of peace and comfort in their later years.

Armando and Rosa don't have this same sense of security. This is in part because Mexico lacks a genuine middle class as many Americans have come to experience it. Although their lives are marked by many of the same milestones with relationships, children, and employment, in spite of their best efforts and hard work, disastrous financial times and political corruption in Mexico have left them with little peace of mind. With the exception of their family, work will define their remaining years.

TWENTY-TWO

Unexpected Farewell

We visit Armando at the highly respected Mayo Clinic; chemotherapy treatments and second chances are readily discussed, but a grim reality infects the room. Through the hospital window, looking out across the lush desert floor, hope still appears realistic. As the sun lies across the majestic McDowell Mountains, brilliant colors wash against the rugged range. Mauricio and Carolina sit close by. My boys balance on his bedside; Armando calls them his "adopted grandchildren." It is April 2008 and our families have suffered and celebrated much during the last decade. He's weak and in great pain, and talks in a whisper. His stomach is no longer grossly bloated, but an overriding fear emanates from his eyes. His belabored breath sends shivers through me. My teeth chatter as I work hard to disguise my fear and discomfort. The scene is all too familiar. We appear to be in the closing act of my own father's painful and delayed death from prostate cancer two years earlier.

Armando is a friend more than a babysitter or nanny. Seeing him in this beleaguered state is uncomfortable. As he struggles to breathe, hundreds of memories wrestle for attention. The two of us have long worked through any differences and grown close over the years. *Not yet*, runs through my mind again and again, *not yet*. Without a shred of guilt I think, *I need you. You can't go yet.*

Better than anyone, he's understood Miguel. "*Dale tiempo, John;*" he counseled me recently to be patient and give Miguel more time through the turbulent teenage years as we sat in the corner of my walk-in shower. Just when I thought we were back on track, I found myself huddled over shattered dreams. My fingers bled as a result of a hasty attempt to clean up shattered glass from a picture frame that my son smashed minutes before in a bout of anger. Now fifteen, Miguel still processes much of life through lenses of rage and opposition. Recognizing defeat on my face, Armando volunteered to clean up. He knew I was spent and ready to give up. "Will the anger ever end?" I asked. But again, Armando talked me off the ledge. "It will be fine, John. It will be fine," he repeated in short, knowing sentences. His voice echoed from the acoustics. "You'll see. You'll see," he said sagely.

To my surprise, my older son takes charge, playing the role of grown up by filling the void within the hospital room with much needed energy. He chats freely with Armando and his children. "*Necesitas agua?*" Miguel gently asks Armando. As he nurses his babysitter, he banters back and forth with Mauricio and Carolina. Miguel tells them stories about his earliest memories of their father. His chatter is a relief to everyone in the room. Perhaps he doesn't sense the critical nature of the situation, or maybe he just wants to cherish every last minute with his friend. Regardless of Miguel's motivation, I'm proud of him. As he talks, Enrique gravitates toward me, apparently sensing his father's discomfort. He sits on my knee and lays his head back against me. We sway gently as I rub his head. My left arm holds him tightly as his heartbeat resonates against my hand. *Lord, bless Armando, ease his pain and stop his suffering,* I pray silently.

"Remember Jim's Junkyard? I love that place," Miguel says genuinely to his drowsy caregiver. Months would go by before I would discover their secret visits to this monster motorcycle junkyard. Located on several acres of industrial land near one of the roughest parts of Phoenix, Miguel had convinced Armando to bring him there to explore thousands of broken down cycles, quads, and off-road vehicles. Their visits would stretch for hours before Armando could convince Miguel to leave. Invariably, they would not go before my son acquired some critical part or piece for his fading red 1981 Honda 70cc three-wheeler, which he's been forever rebuilding. "I am going to work there one day," Miguel whispers to Armando so as not to disturb his sleep. "Let's go again when you feel better, okay?"

"*Donde esta Rosa?*" I whisper to Mauricio. She's recently taken on a new job as nanny for a five year-old boy. Mauricio explains that the boy's mother, a newly divorced single parent, is out of town on business. "She will love your little boy like her own," I had reassured the young mother just a month earlier, when she'd called me for a reference. I was impressed with the woman who seemed well organized and asked many questions. "Would you hire Rosa again to care for your two boys?" she asked. "Absolutely, you'd be crazy not to hire her. I don't think you can find anyone more qualified," I responded. She still seemed hesitant. At the end of our conversation, I encouraged her to meet with Rosa, Armando, and their family, their children being a shining testament to their core values.

Armando wakes but he is too weak to speak. I carry on a conversation with Mauricio and Carolina. Our lives fully entwined, we talk without restraint. Mauricio sits closest to Miguel and encourages him to read *The Secret* by Rhonda Byrne. Mauricio is reading the Spanish translation of the book and as a result is motivated to explore his next great opportunity. After several years of successfully buying and flipping homes during the Phoenix housing boom, the market is in steep decline and Mauricio has been recently forced to take a job as a manager of a discount auto paint shop. "It's just temporary," he chimes in optimistically. "The economy will pick up...it has to."

Mauricio remains focused on my oldest son. "Miguel, you have so much potential but you need to read. I wish I had the mechanical talents you have." Miguel is smiling and nodding, but is still too young to understand the importance of what Mauricio is saying. "If I could do it all over again, I would have stayed in school and studied, studied so much harder. I thought I knew everything. When I got my first car, it was over." As he listens to Mauricio, Miguel holds Armando's hand and rubs it gently, unaware of his small act of kindness. This affection is extraordinary for a teenager who long ago cast aside public signs of fondness from family and friends. "He is really skinny," Enrique whispers in my ear. It's hard for him to see his surrogate grandfather in pain. Innately, Enrique is compassionate and harbors goodness beyond his years. He turns his head into my shirt and quietly cries so no one else will know his sadness.

Carolina and I sit next to one another. She smiles as she looks at Enrique. Our chairs are positioned at the foot of Armando's bed, and we communicate easily through breaks in conversation. She remains beautiful and laughs easily. "How's Don?" I ask. Just like her older sister, she's married an American. He's a real estate agent, another in a small army who had been working to capitalize on what appeared to be an ever-booming housing market. "We're done," she laughs, rubbing her hands together. "We're separated, you didn't hear? I think I am meant to be single," she says with an intentional sense of levity. She finds it healthier to laugh than to have to elaborate on two failed marriages. She mentions, like the economy, that her sister Alejandra's marriage is also falling apart, and her husband's business is unraveling.

Carolina tells me about her job as a sales representative. She is one of two native Spanish speakers in her office. She works mostly with Hispanic clients and spends the majority of her day speaking Spanish. She's thankful to be working but longs for more. She talks fondly of her days as a nanny and stays in close contact with the two girls she cared for from a very young age. On occasion she still baby-sits when the girls' parents are in a bind.

"*Cómo va el fútbol?*" Armando groggily asks the boys, surprising both of them. "*Bien*," Miguel responds gently for both himself and his brother. Miguel still holds his babysitter's hand as Armando drifts back to sleep. "*Es tiempo para su medicina*," a male Hispanic nurse appears at the door, indicating it's time for medicine and announcing that visiting hours are now officially over. My boys and I hug Mauricio and Carolina and one at a time whisper goodnight to our ailing friend.

The nurse slowly turns Armando on his side and gives him a shot of morphine to dull the pain. It's hard to believe that just one month before he was throwing a football in our front yard with my sons and a group of neighborhood kids, one of the smaller ones intent on tackling him. Armando launched a successful pass to Enrique, who scored the winning touchdown just seconds after the boy jumped on Armando's back, attempting to pull him down. The boy had both stick-like arms wrapped tightly around Armando's neck, and his feet tightly wound around his waist. Armando laughed as two other boys successfully tackled him to the ground. In hysterics, he succumbed to a pile of them. One by one I pulled the boys off. As he surfaced, Armando quickly jumped to his feet. Tears ran down his face from laughter as he swatted grass from his shorts and high-fived Enrique. "Good catch," he said in clipped English. "Good boys," Armando said to me as he put his hand on my shoulder, "good boys."

Two weeks after our hospital visit, Alejandra calls and encourages us to come quickly. Death is days, possibly hours away. Hospice has now been substituted for hope. "We're in the wrong place. This is a hotel, not a hospital," Miguel says. He's right; the building does look more like a Holiday Inn than a hospice. "I wonder if they have a pool," Miguel adds as we step away from our car and head to the front entry. Nervous about what awaits, I ignore his comments. "Fairview Nursing Home" the sign reads outside the two-story stucco Southwestern building. As the sliding glass doors disappear, we walk into the lobby. To the right, two women in navy blue scrubs put the final touches on a sparse Dickens Christmas village. The long folding table has a glittery green tablecloth; Christmas lights are taped to the wall with small pieces of gray duct tape. The figurine village is dwarfed by the size of the long table. To our left is a sea of old people, four to a table sitting in the dining room. Most look comatose; a few fiddle with their food. No one is talking. Elvis

Presley's *Blue Christmas* is piped cheerfully throughout the dining room and lobby. For this group of slumping seniors, the volume is loud and seemingly inappropriate.

A sign reading "Hospice" with a red arrow directs us to turn down a long hallway. Enrique grabs my hand as we walk by various rooms with oxygen tanks and IVs affixed to near skeletal figures propped up in hospital beds. I plead with Miguel to slow down and wait for his brother and me. With death lingering, I grow more reticent as we reach the end of the hallway. There are hundreds, thousands of places I would rather be than on this corridor. It's been less than two months since a growth was spotted on Armando's liver; now, metal doors slam loudly shut behind us. The setting ahead does not bespeak second chances. Armando is sixty five and dying.

On the other end of the hallway, a group of Hispanic women whispers softly as they look in our direction. I hold the boys back as I peer into the first room along the hospice wing. I don't recognize the two men who lay motionless in mechanical beds; they both struggle to inhale. The room is frozen and nothing moves. I shake my head "No" as I signal the boys to follow me to the next room. Again, I hold them back at arms distance, while I look. The room is dark. Several women gather around a man closest to the door, while the curtain is pulled around another patient. Clearly invading this family's privacy, I pull out from the doorway and the withering frail man.

"*Pásenle*," Rosa says as she appears in the doorway and signals for us to come in. Her arms are open wide; it's clear she's suffering. It takes me a moment to realize that the ailing man before us is Armando. He's in severe pain and his muscles spasm in agony. He wears a cloth diaper, his bare torso is exposed, and a single sheet covers his lower extremities. He moans from pain and pulls at the sheets as if heat is pouring out from his body. "*Lo siento*," I say over and over to Rosa as we hug one another. Miguel pushes his brother slightly to ensure he's next to console his nanny. As Miguel holds her tightly, Rosa weeps. More than ten years has passed since she first held Miguel and kissed him repeatedly on his cheeks. Now, my teenage son stands toe to toe with his nanny. He's as much a grandson to her as her own children's offspring. Enrique feels uneasy as he quickly hugs Rosa and takes his place at my side. His hand quickly slides into mine. Arm in arm, Rosa and Miguel move closer to Armando. "*Armando – Miguel y Enrique están aquí*," Rosa says softly. Two women stand on the other side of the bed, looking quietly at us. I recognize them from previous family gatherings. One of the women takes over attending to Armando.

I am uncomfortable with death and it shows. I struggle for words and take a secondary position at the foot of Armando's bed. Enrique falls in step and is at my side. I rely on Miguel to comfort and console Rosa. He seems to relish this time and his important role. From nowhere, Armando wakes from his agony and points to me. "*Es Juan*," he says quietly but lucidly. Rosa smiles as she realizes Armando recognizes me and my children. "*Sí, Juan está aquí. Miguel y Enrique también*." She is quick to point to the boys before he quickly fades away.

Rosa works to calm Armando's discomfort by placing both her hands on each side of his face. His pain is crippling but her love is overwhelming. One of the women in the room goes to tell the nurse he needs more medicine. I send both boys out, for they've seen enough. Now alone with Rosa, I'm self-conscious and uncomfortable. With Miguel and Enrique no longer present to buffer the raw emotion and misery, I struggle for words. "*Tenemos muchos recuerdos*." I say simply to Rosa we have many memories. We embrace one final time.

Down the hall, Miguel and Enrique sit on a bench. Miguel stands up as he sees me walking toward them. "Okay guys, it's time to go," I say quietly to the two of them. "No, no I'm not going yet," Miguel pushes past me and heads back to the room. He won't leave until he delivers his own goodbye. He has no intention of missing this final chance, unlike during my dad's final days, when I prevented him and his brother from seeing their grandpa in a compromised state. At his grandfather's funeral, Miguel confronted me after the service. "Why didn't you let me say goodbye?" He could no longer hold back the tears. "Why?" At the time, I thought I was protecting him from death, but in the end I robbed him of closure. As he should, this time around he'll have a chance to say farewell on his terms. Miguel goes directly to Rosa and hugs her. "I love you," he says. "Goodbye," he whispers to Armando, leaning over the hospital bed. He rubs his eyes on his t-shirt, walks past me, and quickly down the hall toward the exit.

Later that day, eight of Enrique's friends meet for his twelfth birthday party at LaserFun. Miguel invites his friend, David. Posted signs in the loud and rowdy lobby advertise an all-night event for teenagers. There are three other rooms filled with boys who look the same age as Enrique, huddled with balloons and streamers.

Fortunately, our party is just two hours long. I feel numb but I feign happiness. I can keep it together for one hundred and twenty minutes. In many ways, I'm glad I'm busy, and my mind occupied. The boys begin their first round of laser tag. Each participant is tracked by a handle—a fake identity; Enrique calls himself, "E-dog". We follow the results of each round on a screen which allots points to the boys for their individual shooting accuracy. A direct laser shot to another nets the shooter points. In between rounds, there are video games and air hockey. Enrique and his friends are animated and enthusiastic; excitement reverberates off the walls. Enrique opens presents; we sing "Happy Birthday"; everyone eats pizza and cupcakes, and drinks Coke. Enrique is in a happy place.

The party provides a respite from the gruesome scenes of the morning. Thankfully, our two-hour time limit comes to an end. Another group of impatient boys and their parents wait for the party room to empty. A young woman, the LaserFun attendant, taps her watch lightly to reinforce it's time for us to clear out. Enrique and his friends pair up and play one final game of air hockey as I gather up presents and any remaining food, which I put back in the ice chest. I smile and joke with parents as they pick up their children. After dozens of these gatherings, I rely on well-rehearsed banter to help me through these transitions. All but one child remains. Enrique's best friend, Colton, will spend the night; they'll play Enrique's new Wii game system. At 10:00 p.m., I announce it is bedtime; tomorrow is the start of a new school week. Colton lies on the bed; Enrique is in a sleeping bag on the floor. Fully clothed, Miguel fell asleep an hour earlier. At 10:30 p.m., the phone rings. Enrique and his friend are laughing in the guest bedroom.

"John, he's gone. My dad has passed away. I thought you would want to know." Alejandra is sad, short, and direct in relaying the message. Although I feel relief that Armando's agony is over, I'm in shock over the brevity of life. The call is rapid and ends abruptly.

"Okay boys, time to calm down," I say as I enter the guest room. Enrique and his buddy are nowhere near sleep. They must talk and giggle amongst themselves for hours before this party will come to an end. "Who was on the phone?" Enrique asks. "Wrong number," I say with my best poker face, unwilling to dampen his happiness.

POSTSCRIPT

Life Lessons

We hold a party in Miguel's honor. It's been ten months, but he's finally home after attending a boarding school in Idaho. Now sixteen, he's handsome and looks grown up. A teenager as well, Enrique has long bangs that cover much of his face. He sits near his grandmother, who ensures he's not overshadowed. A large group gathers around the patio table in the backyard. With each new arrival, the circle of friends and family expands. All eagerly welcome Miguel home.

It's a Saturday afternoon in mid-May, before the arrival of near impossible summer heat that can effortlessly evaporate a crowd. Rosa sits next to my mom and proudly shows photos of grandchildren on her new iPhone. Her thumb nimbly moves the screen from one picture to the next. As the phone circles the table, everyone admires the images. Although the last several years have brought Rosa and her family major obstacles, the images indicate a happy and enduring unit. Now a widow for one year, Rosa forges on. Regal and relaxed, she exudes a pride and confidence that comes from hardship and hope. Her loved ones surround her, which bolsters her sense of accomplishment and optimism for the future.

"*Tú mamá se ve muy bonita,*" Rosa whispers how beautiful my mom looks. She's recovering from surgery for esophageal cancer and wears a short wig. I affectionately call her Twiggy, because she looks hip with her retro hairstyle. Six months earlier, she prevailed through weekly chemotherapy that her doctor would later divulge was suitable for a man close to half her age. Just three months ago, her esophagus was mostly removed and the stomach reattached. Soon after surgery, she weaned herself off a walker and is on her way to a full recovery. Over the last six months, the diagnosis has evolved from tragic to tentatively optimistic. With a new lease on life, albeit a guarded one, she overflows with appreciation and gratitude to be surrounded by family and friends.

The two women reap the benefits of lives lived well. They have an unspoken connection that comes from a set of shared values that guide their actions. Both have overcome adversity, including losing husbands, yet they're far from alone. Having fully dedicated themselves to their families, they're now surrounded on this beautiful afternoon by an extended network of support. Unconditional love is a fundamental testament to explain why family members clamor to be near them. I sit between both and want for nothing.

Playing the reluctant role of pied piper, Enrique gathers a group of Rosa's grandchildren for a game of bocce. They excitedly line up behind him and pretend to march like soldiers in formation to the grassy front yard. He sighs and rolls his eyes as he passes, leaving no doubt he has fully embraced adolescence. A small but poorly hidden smile makes it clear at some level that he enjoys this task.

Rosa is one of a few to understand the journey and our rise through the storm. She beams with pride when she talks of Miguel and Enrique and rightly so, having been mistaken as mother or grandmother no fewer than a hundred times. For so long now, she and her family have been an integral part of the village. Before her, Ana, Carmen, and of course, Paulina laid the foundation.

"*Fuimos al cementerio de Armando.*" In a hushed tone, I share with Rosa that we visited Armando last week after paying our respects to my dad. The two men lie in adjacent cemeteries in a patch of desert now surrounded by tract homes. By the grace of God, the fallout from the housing boom has slowed the inevitable encroachment on their final resting place. My dad is buried in the

Veterans' cemetery. Eventually, my mom will come to rest in this same spot. The images of headstones among the crushed gravel and desert trees with shallow mountain views lingering in the distance brought him a sense of comfort and peace, if not an important distraction in the final painful days before his own death. The Western sunset regularly sits long and wide on his gravesite. His love of this stark and sacred ground remains undeniable.

On our visit, we headed south at the fourth Mesquite tree with black bark and paced fifty yards or so before studying each headstone to locate him. We brought salt and pepper packets from Wendy's and buried them near his headstone. The gift was a tribute to my dad's thriftiness and his overwhelming desire to pass this life lesson onto his grandchildren. Even now, when stopping for fast food, Miguel takes extra packets of sugar, Sweet and Low and salt and pepper, and restocks our pantry. Afterward, we stopped at the newer Catholic cemetery, which borders the fallen soldiers. Armando was cremated and lies within a sleek stone columbarium. "I miss Armando," Miguel said after a quick impromptu prayer. "I really miss our trips to Jim's," he added wistfully, remembering his times at the vast motorcycle junkyard. "He took us on lots of secret trips that were really fun…he was a really cool guy," my younger son added thoughtfully. At the base of the stone memorial, Enrique had a massive bloody nose. It seemed to take forever to locate the bathroom and collect paper towels to mop up after the trail of blood. This was an all too familiar scene, playing out just for Armando, one he witnessed many times in the past.

Daydreaming, I am pulled back into the party by my partner. Most times, Jake is a nervous party host, burdened by the demands of multi-tasking and juggling many balls at once. Best with lists and reminders programmed with technology, a party setting pushes him out of his comfort zone. He's more than happy to play second fiddle. Today, however, he's focused, composed, and fully engaged. He remains calm and stays busy filling drinks and replenishing food trays. He hustles to secure seating for additional family members, and clears the scattered plates from the kids who've long deserted their meals. He provides a status update to parents that all is well with the group of rambunctious kids who now run wildly through the house. Seven years in, he easily interacts with the smallest of party guests in a comfortable tone; gone are the fear and anxiety brought on by little ones. He insists I stay put as I remain seated between my mom and Rosa. He refuses my repeated efforts to help. He's completely dialed into the importance of this moment, well before it strikes me.

There are no two ways about it: Jake is a godsend. My family and friends remind me often that I'm a better person because of him. He appeared in my life just as things were at their worst. More miraculous, he's weathered the storm and now the two of us see a small flicker of what our future holds beyond the trials of parenthood. At this point, I can't imagine life without him.

Once seemingly impossible, the journey is now well underway. As life lessons unfold, at times painfully so, I've never regretted fatherhood or the craziness that makes up our daily routine. Even in the most challenging moments, my decision to adopt two small boys has made me a stronger, wiser, and happier man. Although I have regrets, my complete commitment to the well-being of my boys is not one of them, for in the end, this will be the one thing I got right. As every parent has, I've sacrificed much, but my hope is someday this steadfast commitment will produce a loving extended family that lives well into the future. To see my children grow up happy, loving each other, and contributing positively in this world remains my overriding goal. My parents, as well as the nannies that have passed through our lives, are a testament to this worthy aspiration.

This much is clear—without my kids—I would have been lost in a race distracted by a long list of misdirected ambitions. Parenthood, or life for that matter, is less about enduring a marathon and more about enjoying the moment; less about focusing on what has gone wrong and more about a very long list of what has gone right on any given day. Rosa, and the others before her, reinforced this message. Although basic, this remains one of the hardest life lessons to incorporate day-in and day-out. Each of them had very few material possessions and as a result relied entirely on the composition of their character and core beliefs. Their inherent choice to love and give thanks versus resentment or regret is truly a divine legacy.

Oblivious to the activity around them, Miguel and his friend David sit on stools outside the large circle, eating pizza and laughing. Family and friends are absorbed in one another's company. Rosa looks at Miguel, practically grown, happy and giggling, which makes her grin. In a few short months, Miguel is scheduled to become an Eagle Scout, another milestone, which at one point seemed far from reach. Recognizing his turbulent start and the ongoing challenges, Miguel's future is going to be difficult. However, Rosa and I can't help but acknowledge the moment, knowing the future holds no guarantee. Our shared joy supplants a need to say more or project beyond this day. Our eyes meet again; we smile at one another as we look out at the large collective family before us.

ACKNOWLEDGMENTS

I greatly appreciate the support of my editor, Benee Knauer. Her many constructive suggestions and keen eyes made this a much better book. Special thanks to my extended family for supporting me through the journey of parenthood and the decision to share my story. I am especially grateful to my partner, who upon our first meeting declared that kids made him nervous, but at the end of the day has become a remarkable role model. And finally, to my two sons, who have taught me the true meaning of life. Without them, I would have missed the significance of love.

ABOUT THE AUTHOR

JOHN WALDRON is the father of two sons and makes his home in Phoenix, Arizona with his partner and children. He has taught at several universities and has spent much of his professional life in sales and marketing. He is currently at work on his second book.

CPSIA information can be obtained at www.ICGtesting.com
Printed in the USA
BVOW07s2210100614

355941BV00001BB/5/P